INSIGHT POCKET GUIDE

BEIJING

S0-ARM-370

Discovery
CHANNEL

APA PUBLICATIONS L
Part of the Langenscheidt Publishing Group

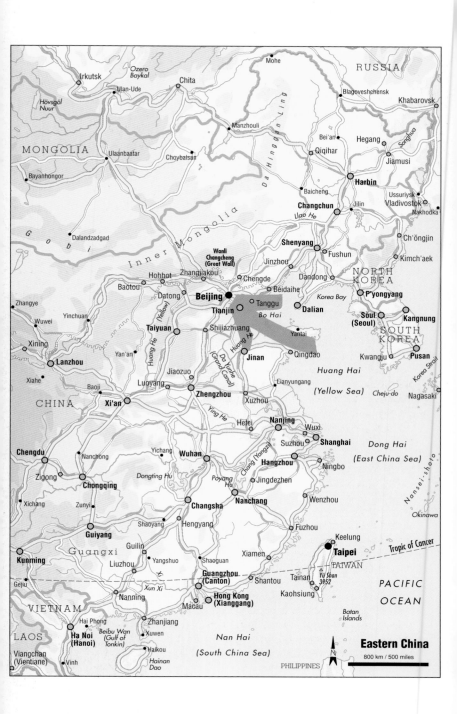

Eastern China

800 km / 500 miles

introduction

Welcome

This guidebook combines the interests and enthusiasms of two of the world's best-known information providers: Insight Guides, who have set the standard for visual travel guides since 1970, and Discovery Channel, the world's premier source of non-fiction television programming. Its aim is to bring you the best of Beijing and its environs in a series of tailor-made itineraries devised by Insight's Beijing correspondent, Kari Huus.

Beijing is all about grandiosity – the Great Wall, the Forbidden City, Tiananmen Square and the Temple of Heaven. It is, after all, the capital for one-fifth of the world's population. Throughout the centuries, every ruler has moulded the city in his own image, creating layer upon layer of architectural statements spanning centuries. But Beijing is also a series of villages that creep between and sprawl beyond the halls of power. In the various *hutong (*alleyways) of the city, life comprises myriad wonderful little traditions – like raising crickets and flying kites. To help you cover these fascinating contrasts, the author has put together 10 itineraries that cover Beijing and its surroundings. The full-day day itineraries include all the major highlights while the shorter tours take in a variety of historical sites, temples, parks, markets and myriad *hutong.*

There are also three excursions to places further afield: the famous Great Wall and Ming Tombs; Bedaihe beach, where China's top brass hobnob; and Chengde, an old imperial summer retreat. The carefully-devised itineraries in this book anticipate the vagaries of travel in China and offer good old-fashioned advice on how to cope. Chapters on shopping, eating out and nightlife, and a useful practical information section on travel essentials complete this reader-friendly guide.

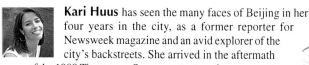

Kari Huus has seen the many faces of Beijing in her four years in the city, as a former reporter for Newsweek magazine and an avid explorer of the city's backstreets. She arrived in the aftermath of the 1989 Tiananmen Square protests and was present throughout its dramatic wave of economic reform. 'It feels like I've been living in several different places at the same time. The mood and the landscape of the city keep changing,' she says, 'depending on your vantage point.' A fluent speaker of Mandarin, Huus knows people as diverse as communist officials, playwrights and bicycle repairmen. She brings a keen insight and enthusiasm to this book, filled with details that bring this historically rich and quirky capital to life.

6   **contents**

Pages 2/3: the Summer Palace
Pages 8/9: Nine Dragon Screen, Beihai Park

History & Culture

T he well-worn image of Chairman Mao standing on Tiananmen Gate (Gate of Heavenly Peace) and proclaiming the founding of the People's Republic of China, is symbolic of Beijing's emergence as the modern capital of this vast country. Throughout China's history the city's rise has been violent and uncertain. Only after many cycles of destruction and reconstruction did the former garrison town become the political and cultural centre of the Middle Kingdom.

Frontier Days

The discovery of the skull of the Peking Man near Beijing in 1929 proved that prehistoric humans settled here more than 500,000 years ago. Yet little more is known until about 5,000 years ago, by which time neolithic agricultural villages had been established within the area of the modern city. The recorded history of the city begins around 1000BC, when it was a trading town called Ji. Its strategic location, on the border of the agricultural plains to the south and the open steppes to the north, made it a garrison town which changed hands repeatedly between the warring kingdoms of the north.

Qin Shi Huangdi, the first emperor of the Qin dynasty, unified China in 221BC, making Ji a part of one of the world's largest empires. He was obsessed with protecting China's northern frontier, and connected walls built by previous kingdoms to form the Great Wall. The massive project was continued by successive rulers using conscript labour, but Ji was often raided by northern tribes. During the Liao dynasty (AD 916–1125), the city was renamed Yanjing and in the 12th century was referred to as Zhongdu (Central Capital). The city underwent another transformation when 'barbarian' conquerors from the north, the Mongols who founded the Yuan dynasty in the 13th century, proclaimed Zhongdu as the capital of the new dynasty.

Mongol Conquest and Rule

When Genghis Khan's armies stormed Beijing in 1215, the month-long invasion was the most brutal yet. The court's treasures were looted and the city was razed. But it was from these ashes that arose one of the world's greatest capitals. By 1279, Genghis Khan's grandson, Kublai Khan, ruled not only all of China but also much of the Eurasian land mass, from parts of Vietnam and Burma to the Baltic Sea. But, like many before him and since, Kublai Khan was as much conquered by Chinese culture as he was the conqueror of its territory. He was fascinated by Buddhism and China's advanced knowledge of astronomy and agriculture.

Left: terracotta warriors, Xi'an, from the Qin dynasty
Right: print of Qin Shi Huangdi, Qin dynasty

Kublai Khan's capital, then known as Dadu (Great Capital) in Chinese and Khan Balik (City of the Khan) in Mongolian, was built on the present site of Beijing. Because of a lack of educated Mongol officials, his administrators were mostly Chinese; his capital a copy of traditional Chinese capitals.

This was the city that impressed Marco Polo, who for 17 years served at the court of the Khan. The Italian merchant, fresh from medieval Europe, was impressed that Dadu was laid out with the precision of a chessboard, with broad and straight streets lined with fine courtyard homes and inns. Hostels in the suburbs, and some 20,000 prostitutes, served merchants from all over the world. In the city centre, on the site of today's Beihai Park, stood Kublai Khan's palace surrounded by a 6½-km (4-mile) wall.

The Mongols improved roads and canals, leading to an increase in both regional and international trade. By the end of Kublai Khan's reign in 1293, the Tonghua Canal had been completed, linking the capital with the Grand Canal. Dadu's population had grown to around 500,000.

Like their counterparts in previous dynasties, later Yuan officials and civil servants became increasingly corrupt and inept. The Mongols exported much of China's wealth to other parts of their kingdom, and starvation was widespread. Heavy taxes were levied on citizens who were not of Mongol descent. No longer faced with a shortage of educated personnel, the Mongol rulers excluded Chinese from government posts, choosing Mongols or foreigners instead. The Chinese had become third-class citizens in their own country, behind the Mongols and their central Asian allies. Not surprisingly, in 1368, an army of impoverished Chinese peasants overthrew the Yuan dynasty and brought about the end of Mongol rule in China.

The Ming Dynasty

With the founding of the Ming dynasty (1368–1644), the Chinese were again masters of a unified China. The new rulers moved their capital to Nanjing, in the heart of a rich agricultural region to the south. But, with an eye to expand China's territory northward, Ming Emperor Yongle soon moved the capital back to its previous location, naming it Beijing (Northern Capital).

Emperor Yongle's reign (1403–25) was the cultural pinnacle of imperial Beijing, particularly in architecture. The Imperial Palace, also known as the Forbidden City, was constructed under Yongle and has remained symbolic of Beijing's pre-eminence ever since. Tiananmen Gate, now adorned with Mao's portrait, is also a legacy of that period. So is another of the city's most striking structures, the Temple of Heaven (Tiantan), where the emperor communed with the gods twice yearly. Yongle also rebuilt Kublai Khan's city walls around the imperial city and added another rectangle encompassing the Temple of Heaven in the south.

Above: Kublai Khan ruled from 1271 until 1294
Right: an early view of the Imperial Palace

Throughout the Ming dynasty, emperors mobilised huge armies of labourers to fortify the Great Wall. Much of it was rebuilt, and many new towers and some whole sections were added, especially near Beijing. More than 200 years of continuous construction resulted in a 3,000-km (1,900-mile) wall.

Soon after Emperor Yongle's death, however, China closed itself to the outside world and forbade its people to emigrate or explore foreign lands. Foreigners were, by and large, despised for their barbarian ways. The Chinese also rejected Western science, which had just begun to revolutionise the outside world. This paranoia and insecurity led to a slowdown of China's development in areas such as astronomy and navigation, in which it had once been a world leader.

Each successive emperor became increasingly enmeshed in elaborate palace ceremonies and isolated from the outside world. Palace eunuchs became corrupt and powerful, siphoning riches from the palace and extracting heavy taxes from the poor. They controlled information to the emperor so that news of peasant rebellions did not always reach him. Not surprisingly, another peasant uprising toppled the Ming dynasty in 1644 and paved the way for an invasion from the northeast, by the Manchus, 43 days later.

The Qing Dynasty

Unlike the invaders before them, the Manchus who founded the Qing dynasty (1644–1911) did not destroy the city they occupied. Prolific builders and renovators, the Qing rulers built lavish palaces, mixing the styles of past dynasties, often with gaudy results. Many of the 800 or so pavilions, palaces and temples built by the Ming were preserved into the 20th century. Most of the relics in Beijing date from the 600 years of Ming and Qing rule.

The Qing emperors tried to grapple with the problems that had toppled the Ming. They maintained the examination system for choosing officials, slashed the number of eunuchs to minimise court intrigue and tried to reform the tax system. By far the most colourful character was Qianlong (1736–99), the longest reigning Chinese emperor. He was a despot who ruthlessly suppressed intellectuals suspected of disloyalty. But he loved the arts and was respon-

history/culture

sible for some of the city's more flamboyant architectural details. The exquisite arts collection at the Imperial Palace is due mainly to Qianlong's intense passion for the arts.

The drive for expansion that began with the Ming dynasty's Yongle carried on into the Qing dynasty and became the main focus of their 267-year reign. Under Emperor Qianlong, Chinese territory expanded dramatically northwards and westwards. By the end of the 19th century, Beijing ruled over four times as much territory as it had during the Ming dynasty.

End of Empire

While China was expanding in the 18th and 19th centuries, Western colonial powers were changing the face of the globe. Beijing became increasingly suspicious of the outside world. Foreign trade was limited to Guangzhou (Canton) and frustrated by complex regulations. The British, who were keen to acquire better access to the Chinese market, sent a high-level delegation in 1793 to the Chinese port of Tianjin, aboard a warship loaded with expensive gifts and state-of-the-art technology. But Emperor Qianlong rebuffed the British with an edict to King George III, saying that China did not need to trade with Britain because she 'already possessed everything a civilised people could ever want'. Britain's request to set up a consulate in Beijing was also rejected.

But Britain would not take no for an answer. Backed by military force, foreign traders pressed shipments of opium on the Chinese market to offset Britain's growing trade deficit. The First Opium War of 1839–42 forced the palace to allow foreign governments extra-territoriality in an area just outside the palace gates. By the end of the Second Opium War in 1860, the emperor had fled to Chengde while Western troops destroyed a large swathe of the city, including the old Summer Palace. The rulers' impotence infuriated the Chinese; secret societies sprang up and small-scale rebellions became common.

In the final days of the Qing dynasty, the palace was a fortress against the reality of China's decay and the stage where the last court tragedy was acted out. The emperor's favourite concubine, Empress Cixi, rose to eminence after a power struggle in the palace in 1861. She dominated and terrorised the court, but could not hold the crumbling kingdom together.

In 1900, a secret society called the Boxers laid siege to the Foreign Legation Quarter for 50 days and Empress Cixi was forced to flee. Before her death in 1908, she installed three-year-old Pu Yi on the throne, who was to be the last of China's emperors. His story is told in the 1988 movie, *The Last Emperor*.

Above: Pu Yi as a young child

history/culture

The Republican Era

In 1911, a revolution led by Dr Sun Yat-sen attempted to launch China into the modern world and restore the country to its people. It ended imperial rule, but the old problems of feuding warlords, poverty, factionalism and foreign invasion continued for another 30 years.

At the end of World War I, Western powers continued to carve up China for themselves. The Treaty of Versailles ceded Chinese territory to the Japanese, humiliating China. The reaction to this marked a turning point in the Chinese people's psyche: students and intellectuals around the country took to the streets in what came to be known as the May Fourth Movement of 1919, demanding independence and territorial integrity.

In 1927, the Nationalist Party (Kuomingtang), under Chiang Kai-shek, tried to unify China again by force. On 10 October 1928, it formally founded the Republic of China (ROC) with its capital in Nanjing. In the countryside, the Chinese Communist Party (CCP), founded in Shanghai in 1921 and led by the young Mao Zedong, waged a guerrilla war against the new government. But the Japanese occupation of China soon forced the Nationalists and the Communists to form an uneasy alliance that lasted until the end of World War II. In the bitter civil war that followed, the Communists were victorious and Chiang Kai-shek and two million other Nationalists fled to Taiwan.

Communist China

In true imperial style, Mao Zedong declared the founding of the People's Republic of China (PRC) from Tiananmen Gate on 1 October 1949, restoring Beijing as the capital. The new leaders took to their task with zeal, redistributing land to the peasants, and undertaking massive industrialisation projects. In Beijing, slums were razed, and new Soviet-style factories, offices, apartment blocks and universities built. In 1957, most of the city walls, hundreds of temples and historical sites were demolished as 12,000 'volunteers' worked at breakneck speed to complete Tiananmen Square and the gargantuan buildings surrounding it in time for the PRC's 10th anniversary.

But the euphoria was followed by a series of political campaigns that left deep scars on the whole nation. The Anti-Rightist Movement of 1957 targeted intellectuals, capitalists and other 'class enemies'. Hot on its heels was the Great Leap Forward (1958–60), a disastrous attempt at overnight modernisation that led to mass starvation in the countryside.

However, the most devastating mass movement was the Cultural Revolution (1966–76). Millions of young zealots were mobilised to wage war on feudal and bourgeois culture. Many people were denounced as traitors or class enemies and lost their jobs, possessions, liberty and often their lives. Young people and educated adults from Beijing and other urban areas were also sent to the countryside to 'learn from the peasants'. Most

Right: Mao Zedong proclaims the founding of the People's Republic of China, 1949

had no idea when or if they would be allowed to return. Fear and chaos reigned until Mao's death in September 1976. In the last years of his life, the notorious Gang of Four, led by Mao's wife, Jiang Qing, used the movement to seize power. The death of Premier Zhou Enlai in January 1976, a moderating force in the government, sparked mass mourning in Beijing that turned into an outcry for change. Later that year, the Gang of Four were arrested and tried. The two perceived leaders of the group – Jiang Qing and Zhang Chunqiao – were given suspended death sentences and the remaining two members received lengthy prison terms.

Reform Years

After Mao's death, Beijing struggled to modernise. Communist ideology was gradually discarded for pragmatic economic reform under Deng Xiaoping's leadership in the years following 1978. China began to open up and there was more contact with foreigners. The rigid bureaucracy gave way, at least in the economic sphere, to a more freewheeling society.

But these policies involved a delicate balancing act, more evident in Beijing than elsewhere. In 1979, the Democracy Wall movement brought millions onto the streets, calling for greater political freedom. In 1986, a

democratic movement in the central Chinese city of Hefei sparked protests in Beijing and Shanghai. Both events, led by students and intellectuals, were followed by greater repression of the press, arts and political reformers. In 1989, millions of students and workers marched to Tiananmen Square to protest against corruption and appeal for political reform.

When the military moved in to quell the protests on June 4, several hundred demonstrators died and a pall of silence fell over the city. As troops lined the Dongchang'an Jie, Beijing's future seemed bleak. Political reform was ruled out and economic reform seemed threatened. But in 1992, party elder Deng Xiaoping made a highly publicised tour of the booming southern provinces where his reforms had taken hold. The idea of the socialist market economy, accredited to Deng, became the core of government and party policy by March 1993. Deng's logic was that if some people became rich, then the rest would take care of itself. After his death in 1997, the torch of economic reform passed to his successor, Jiang Zemin, who has maintained the pace of economic development since.

The historic, but controversial, decision to award Beijing the 2008 Olympic Games is set to spur the city to yet more growth and investment in the coming years. It is hoped that this, in turn, will lead to improvements in human rights and political stability in China.

Above: the 1989 demonstrations in Tiananmen Square shook China and the world

HISTORY HIGHLIGHTS

1030–221BC: The city of Ji develops on the site of Beijing.

221–207BC: Emperor Qin Shi Huangdi unifies China and begins Great Wall.

200BC–AD1200: Beijing becomes a strategic garrison town between warring kingdoms.

1215: Mongols led by Genghis Khan overrun Beijing.

1260: Kublai Khan founds the Mongol (Yuan) dynasty.

1271: Kublai Khan establishes the capital of Dadu (Khan Balik) at Beijing. Marco Polo visits China, and serves at the court of the Khan for 17 years.

1368–1644 The Ming dynasty.

1400s: Forbidden City and most of the existing Great Wall built.

1644–1911: Qing (Manchu) dynasty is established.

1839–42: The First Opium War.

1860: The Second Opium War.

1861–1908: Empress Cixi holds power.

1900: Boxer Rebellion lays siege to the Foreign Legation Quarter.

1911: Revolution headed by Sun Yat-sen ends imperial rule.

1919: Treaty of Versailles cedes territory to Japan and sparks May Fourth Movement for democracy and sovereignty.

1921: The Chinese Communist Party is founded in Shanghai.

1928: The Nationalist government establishes its capital in Nanjing.

1935: Communists embark on the Long March to escape Nationalist forces.

1937: The Marco Polo Bridge incident precedes a full-scale invasion by the Japanese, who occupy much of China until the end of World War II.

1949: Mao Zedong declares the founding of the People's Republic of China. Beijing becomes the capital.

1957–59: Tiananmen Square and surrounding monoliths built. Most of the city wall is demolished.

1957: The Anti-Rightist Movement singles out 300,000 intellectuals for criticism, punishment or imprisonment.

1958: Mao launches the disastrous Great Leap Forward.

1959–62: Famine claims 20 million.

1960: Beijing and Moscow split, beginning two decades of Cold War.

1966–76: Cultural Revolution leads to widespread persecution, chaos and near economic collapse.

1972: President Nixon visits Beijing, first official contact between US and PRC.

1976: Premier Zhou Enlai and Chairman Mao die. Gang of Four arrested.

1978: Premier Deng Xiaoping launches economic reforms.

1979: Democracy Wall Movement quashed.

1980: Gang of Four tried on nationwide television. Reforms are effected.

1989: Soviet President Mikhail Gorbachev visits Beijing.

1989: Tiananmen Square democracy demonstration is crushed by military.

1992: Japanese Emperor Akihito visits China. Deng Xiaoping tours South.

1993: China's parliament officially endorses market economy and begins a series of structural reforms to its finanical, currency and taxation systems.

1997: Deng Xiaoping dies. Hong Kong returns to China. President Jiang Zemin consolidates power.

1998: President Clinton visits China. China suffers worst flood in a century.

1999: China celebrates 50th anniversary of its founding. Macau returns to China. Policy established to speed up the development of western China.

2001: US-Chinese relations are strained when a US spy plane collides with a Chinese fighter jet in Chinese airspace. Beijing is chosen ahead of Toronto and Paris as host city for the 2008 Olympic Games.

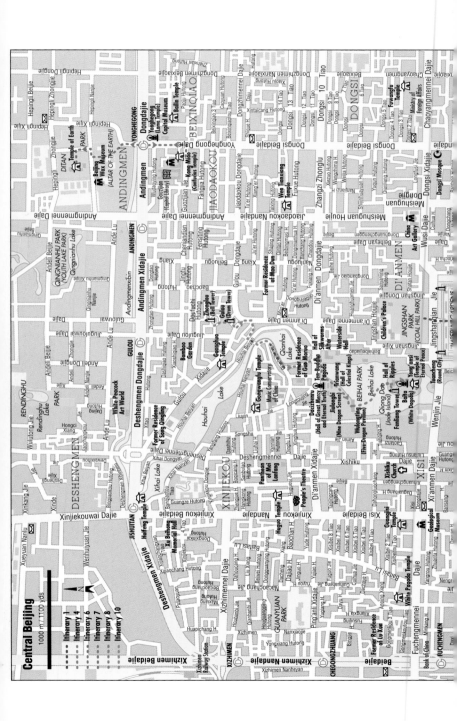

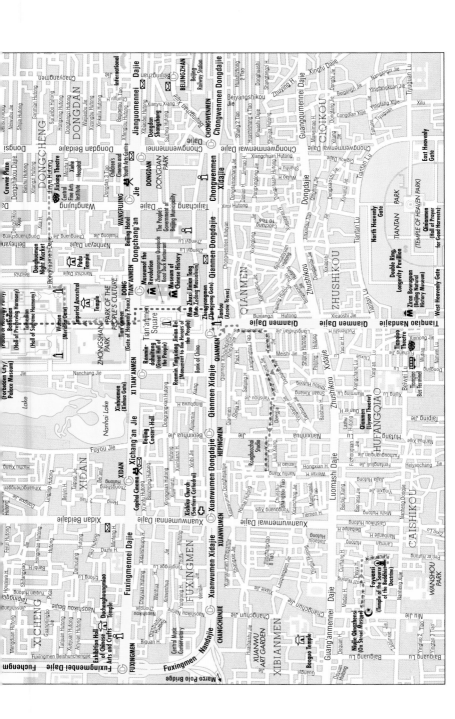

Beijing
& Environs

Beijing is the capital and political nerve centre of China, but it's far from the geographical centre. Located on the northern plain 180km (112 miles) from the ocean, it suffers bitter winters and blistering summers. The good news is that, despite being home to more than 12 million people, it is less congested than most other large Chinese cities.

Beijing municipality covers 16,808sq km (6,488sq miles), so sightseeing entails covering a lot of ground. The city is laid out on a grid, with Dongchang'an Jie (Avenue of Eternal Peace) dividing the city into the northern and southern sections. Street names change according to their relationship to the gates of the former city wall. Dongchang'an Jie, for example, turns into Fuxingmennei meaning 'inside Fuxing Gate' to the west and Fuxingmenwai or 'outside Fuxing Gate' further west. Four ring roads loop around the city, and a fifth has been proposed.

Taxis and bicycles are the best forms of transport in Beijing. Taxis are numerous and reasonably priced. The subway is useful for getting to the general vicinity of your destination; buses are recommended on some routes, but both tend to be very crowded. Bicycles are a good way to see the city and can be rented at many hotels or in front of the Scitech Plaza shopping centre, opposite the Friendship Store on Jianguomenwai.

Exploring the City

The following 10 itineraries take in Beijing's world-famous sights, starting with Tiananmen Square and the Imperial Palace (the Forbidden City). The first two itineraries take a full day each. Itineraries 3 to 8 are shorter, mostly taking a half-day to complete. Itineraries 9 and 10 are evening tours.

The itineraries are punctuated with temples, parks and museums, but also lead you through the city's maze of alleyways (*hutong*) to some interesting neighbourhoods and markets. By big city standards, Beijing is remarkably safe, friendly and inexpensive, so take the listed suggestions as jump-off points for your own explorations. Any free time you have will not be wasted – simply walk the city's streets and turn down any *hutong* you happen to come across. Beijing is a city of walls; only exploring beyond them and into the various *hutong* can you see the traditional life of Beijingers. Each and every corner holds the possibility of a unique experience.

There are also three longer excursions out of the city, which take in the Great Wall and Ming Tombs, Bedaihe beach resort and the great mountain retreat of the Qing emperors, Chengde.

Left: the Imperial Palace
Right: a stone lion stands guard

1. TIANANMEN SQUARE, IMPERIAL PALACE AND JINGSHAN PARK *(see maps, pages 23 and 24)*

A front door to back door trek through the imperial heart of the city, leading through Tiananmen Square, the Imperial Palace and the gardens of Jingshan Park. This is a full day tour.

Take the subway to the Qianmen stop. You can also reach Tiananmen by public bus Nos 1, 4, 10, 20, 52, 57, 120 and 802.

A first day of exploring Beijing starts logically enough at **Qianmen** (Front Gate). This tower (open daily 8am–4pm; free) is the largest of nine similar gates in the wall that used to embrace the Inner City, which has at its centre, the Imperial Palace or Forbidden City. Qianmen, built in 1419, was destroyed during the Boxer Rebellion of 1900 and rebuilt in 1905. The front gate provides a great vantage point for studying the layout of old Beijing.

The north section of Qianmen, across the street, is called **Zhengyangmen** (Main Gate) while Qianmen's southern gate is **Jianlou** (Arrow Tower), built in 1439 to serve as a watchtower. The Outer City, which was also enclosed by a high wall, extends southward. The bustling, narrow streets to the south form the lively Dazhalan shopping district *(see Itinerary 5)*, which at the end of the 19th century teemed with decadent pleasures for off-duty officials. Further south is the Temple of Heaven *(see Itinerary 3)*.

The north side of Qianmen overlooks **Tiananmen Square**, in the middle of which stands an obelisk. To the left stands the Great Hall of the People and to the right the Museum of Chinese History and Revolution; in the centre is the Mao Zedong Mausoleum. At the far end of the square, across Dongchang'an Jie, is Tiananmen Gate, or the Gate of Heavenly Peace, leading the way to the Imperial Palace, now officially known as the Palace Museum (Gugong). To the immediate west of Tiananmen Gate is the entrance to Zhongshan (Sun Yat-sen) Park, dedicated to the early Nationalist leader. The park used to be part of the palace, as did Zhongnanhai, a little further west, where China's top leaders now live. To the northwest you will see the white dagoba in Beihai Park, once part of the imperial gardens.

Views of the Past

Before leaving Qianmen, visit the photo exhibition inside. There are wonderful views of Beijing at the turn of the century, from cricket fighting to camel caravans arriving at the city gate. Next, join the queue to pay your respects at the **Mao Zedong Mausoleum** (Mao Zhuxi Jinian Tang; open Mon, Wed and Fri 8–11.30am and 2–4pm; Tues, Thurs and Sat 8–11.30am; free), completed in 1977, a year after his death. Even today, when the little red book of Mao quotations is long past its sell-by date, people from all over China visit his mausoleum, filing reverently past his embalmed body in its glass sarcophagus. Entrance is free, but you must leave

Left: Tiananmen guard
Top right: the Great Hall of the People

your bag at the door. Though the queue looks daunting, visitors are hustled through quickly. Just outside the mausoleum, you get a graphic picture of how socialism is fast becoming mere consumer kitsch, as people are ushered through a small bazaar selling Chairman Mao busts, bags, badges and musical lighters playing *The East is Red*.

Memorials and Museums

The 37m (121ft) obelisk that you saw earlier in the centre of Tiananmen Square is called the **Monument to the People's Heroes** (Renmin Yingxiong Jinian Bei), dedicated in 1958 to those who died for the country. The bas relief on the pedestal portrays the struggle from the First Opium War (1839–42) to the founding of the PRC in 1949. Start on the east side and move clockwise to see it chronologically.

Next, visit the **Great Hall of the People** (Renmindahuitang; open daily 8.30am–3pm except during meetings; entrance fee), officially opened in 1959, where China's parliament, the National People's Congress, meets and other important conferences and diplomatic meetings take place. One room of the hall is dedicated to each of China's 32 provinces and regions. If you enjoy political history, cross the square to the imposing Stalinist-style **Museum of Chinese History and Revolution** (Zhongguo Geming Lishi

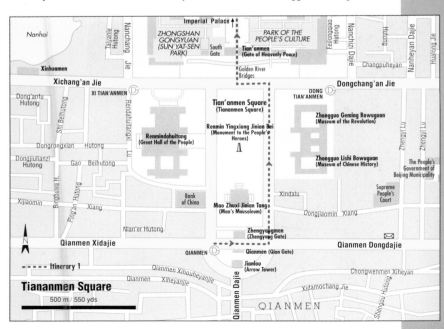

Tiananmen Square

500 m / 550 yds

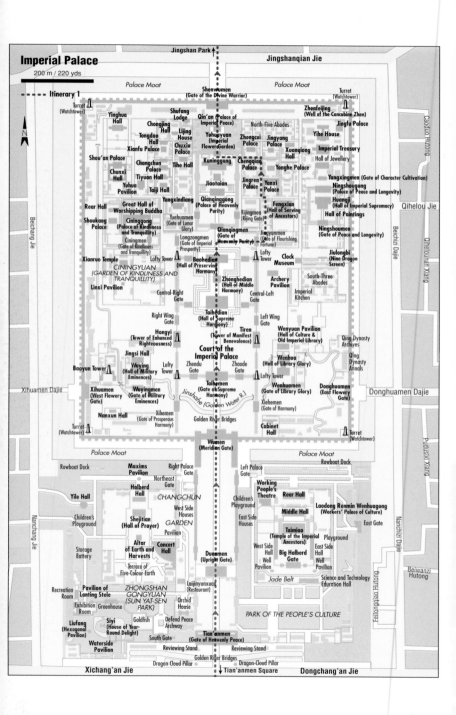

Imperial Palace

200 m / 220 yds

- - - - Itinerary 1

Jingshan Park ↑

Jingshanqian Jie

Palace Moat

Palace Moat

Shenwumen
(Gate of the Divine Warrior)

Turret
(Watchtower)

Turret
(Watchtower)

Caodou Hutong

Yinghua
Hall

Shufang
Lodge

Qin'an (Palace of
Imperial Peace)

Zhenfeijing
(Well of the Concubine Zhen)

North-Five Abodes

Jingfu Palace

Chongjing
Hall

Lijing
House

Yuhuayuan
(Imperial
FlowerGarden)

Zhongcui
Palace

Jingyang
Palace

Yihe House

Tongdao
Hall

Chuxiu
Palace

Xuanyuan
Hall

Imperial Treasury

Xianfu Palace

Tihe Hall

Chengqian
Palace

Yonghe Palace

Hall of Jewellery

Shou'an Palace

Changchun
Palace

Kuninggong

Yangxingmen (Gate of Character Cultivation)

Chunxi
Hall

Tiyuan Hall

Jiaotaian

Jingren
Palace

Yanxi
Palace

Ningshougong
(Palace of Peace and Longevity)

Yuhua
Pavilion

Taiji Hall

Fengxian
(Hall of Serving
of Ancestors)

Huangji
(Hall of Imperial Supremacy)

Qihelou Jie

Rear Hall

Great Hall of
Worshipping Buddha

Yangxiandiang

Qianqinggong
(Palace of Heavenly
Purity)

Rijingmen
(Rising Gate)

Hall of Paintings

Shoukang
Palace

Cininggong
(Palace of Kindliness
and Tranquility)

Yuehuamen
(Gate of Lunar
Glory)

Qianqingmen
(Gate of
Heavenly Purity)

Jingyunmen
(Gate of Flourishing
Fortune)

Ningshoumen
(Gate of Peace and Longevity)

Beichang Jie

Ciningmen
(Gate of Kindliness
and Tranquility)

Longzongmen
(Gate of Imperial
Prosperity)

Xianruo Temple

Lofty Tower

Baohedian
(Hall of Preserving
Harmony)

Lofty
Tower

Clock
Museum

Jiulongbi
(Nine Dragon
Screen)

Beizhai Dajie

CININGYUAN
(GARDEN OF KINDLINESS AND
TRANQUILITY)

Zhonghedian
(Hall of Middle
Harmony)

Archery
Pavilion

South-Three
Abodes

Qihelou Xiang

Linxi Pavilion

Central-Right
Gate

Central-Left
Gate

Imperial
Kitchen

Taihedian
(Hall of Supreme
Harmony)

Right Wing
Gate

Left Wing
Gate

Hongyi
(Tower of Enhanced
Righteousness)

Tiren
(Tower of Manifest
Benevolence)

Wenyuan Pavilion
(Hall of Culture &
Old Imperial Library)

Qing Dynasty
Archives

Jingsi Hall

Court of the
Imperial Palace

Wenhua
(Hall of Library Glory)

Qing
Dynasty
Annals

Baoyun Tower

Wuying
(Hall of Military
Eminences)

Lofty
Tower

Zhendu
Gate

Zhaode
Gate

Wenhuamen
(Gate of Library Glory)

Donghuamen
(East Flowery
Gate)

Donghuamen Dajie

Xihuamen
(West Flowery
Gate)

Wuyingmen
(Gate of Military
Eminences)

Lofty Tower

Nanxun Hall

Xihemen
(Gate of Prosperous
Harmony)

Taihemen
(Gate of Supreme
Harmony)

Jinshahe (Golden Water R.)

Xiehemen
(Gate of Harmony)

Cabinet
Hall

Turret
(Watchtower)

Golden River Bridges

Turret
(Watchtower)

Palace Moat

Wumen
(Meridian Gate)

Palace Moat

Rowboat Dock

Right Palace
Gate

Left Palace
Gate

Rowboat Dock

Maxims
Pavilion

Working
People's
Theatre

Rear Hall

Yile Hall

Halberd
Hall

Northeast
Gate

CHANGCHUN

Children's
Playground

Middle Hall

Laodong Renmin Wenhuagong
(Workers' Palace of Culture)

Nanchang Jie

Children's
Playground

Shejitian
(Hall of Prayer)

West Side
Houses

GARDEN

Pavilion

East Side
Houses

Taimiao
(Temple of the Imperial
Ancestors)

East Gate

Nanchizi Dajie

Storage
Battery

Altar
of Earth and
Harvests

Concert
Hall

West Side
Hall

East Side
Hall

Playground

Terrace of
Five-Colour Earth

Duanmen
(Upright Gate)

Big Halberd
Gate

Well
Pavilion

Well
Pavilion

Recreation
Room

Pavilion of
Lanting Stele

ZHONGSHAN
GONGYUAN
(SUN YAT-SEN
PARK)

Laijinyunxuai
(Restaurant)

Jade Belt

Science and Technology
Education Hall

Feilongqiao Hutong

Beiwanzi
Hutong

Exhibition
Room

Greenhouse

Orchid
House

PARK OF THE PEOPLE'S CULTURE

Liufang
(Hexagonal
Pavilion)

Siyi
(House of Year-
Round Delight)

Goldfish

Defend Peace
Archway

Pudusi Xiang

Waterside
Pavilion

South Gate

Tian'anmen
(Gate of Heavenly Peace)

Xichang'an Jie

Reviewing Stand

Reviewing Stand

Dongchang'an Jie

Golden River Bridges

Dragon-Cloud Pillar

Dragon-Cloud Pillar

Tian'anmen Square

Right: Tiananmen Gate, with Mao's portrait

Bowuguan; open daily 8.30am–4.30pm; entrance fee). Supported by 11 columns, a vast entrance hall connects the two wings. To the right is the **Museum of Chinese History**, which covers the entire history of China, and has many ancient and unique cultural relics. Recently renovated, it is the best history museum in the capital by Beijing standards. The exhibits cover all periods of China's long history with an impressive and comprehensive display of objects, including bronzes, pottery, sculpture and other works of art. Often, the museum has special exhibitions as well.

The left wing houses the **Museum of the Chinese Revolution**, with photographs, paintings, documents and relics representing the key events and personalities that brought communism to China. As the interpretation of history is politically sensitive, the museum was closed for most of the Cultural Revolution. It was also briefly closed in 1989, when soldiers occupied it during the protests in Tiananmen Square.

The Great Meeting Place

Relax awhile in **Tiananmen Square**. In Ming and Qing times two rows of ministry offices stood on this site. When the emperor wanted to hand down an edict, he would pass with great fanfare to deliver it to the Ministry of Rites, where it was recopied and distributed throughout the empire. The old ministries and many other buildings were demolished to make Tiananmen larger than any other public square, including Moscow's Red Square. The area has been the venue for anti-government demonstrations, mass rallies and parades both before and since the building of the square. Now it's a convenient place for locals to meet and show off kite-flying, soccer or photography skills. After being closed for much of 1999 for renovation, Tiananmen Square is now graced with strips of green grass, part of the Beijing government's efforts at beautifying the city in time for the 2008 Olympics.

Before moving on to the Imperial Palace, take a pedicab to the nearby **Beijing Hotel** (33 Dongchang'an Jie; tel: 10-6513 7766) for lunch. Try the *gongbao jiding*, diced chicken with chillies and peanuts, at its moderately

priced **Sichuan Restaurant** (open daily 11.30am–2pm; 6.30–9.30pm) in the hotel's old section. Or go to one of the Mongolian hotpot restaurants in the alleys near Qianmen. These are easy to spot from the eye-catching hot-pot pictures you'll see in their windows.

After lunch, return to the **Tiananmen Gate** (Gate of Heavenly Peace), to enter **Imperial Palace** where China's revolutionary and feudal legacies converge. The gate, built in 1417 and restored in 1651, is now adorned with Mao's portrait and the slogans: 'Long live the People's Republic of China' and 'Long live the great union of the peoples of the world'. It was here that Mao announced the founding of the PRC before a crowd of 300,000 in 1949.

The Imperial Palace

From Tiananmen Gate, a long approach takes you through a second gate before reaching the **Imperial Palace** (open daily 8.30am–4.30pm; entrance fee). Whether referred to by its official Chinese name of **Palace Museum** (Gugong) or its more well-known Western sobriquet, the Forbidden City, this is a sight you should not miss. A useful and informative audio guide, available in eight languages, can be rented for a guided tour of the palace's main buildings. Visitors can move at their own pace between signposted and numbered points. Actor Roger Moore reads the English commentary. To collect an audio guide, enter the Imperial Palace through glass doors to the right of the main entrance.

Behind walls more than 10m (30ft) high, and within the 50m (160ft) moat, life in the palace was dictated by complex rules and rituals. Entrance was denied to ordinary people, but the gigantic gateway leads today's tourists to a fascinating display of Chinese cultural history in what is probably the best-preserved site of classical Chinese architecture.

In 1421, after 17 years of construction, the Ming Emperor Yongle moved into the palace. Up to the founding of the republic in 1911 – a period covering the reign of 24 emperors from the Ming dynasty until the last emperor, Puyi – the palace was the imperial residence and centre of the Middle Kingdom. It has 9,000 rooms in which an estimated 8,000 to 10,000 people lived,

including 3,000 eunuchs, as well as maids and concubines, all within an area of 70 hectares (180 acres).

The entire site can be divided into two large areas: **Waichao**, the Outer Court, in the south, and in the rear, **Neiting**, the Inner Residence. Through the middle runs the imperial walkway, decorated with finely carved stone dragon and phoenix bas-reliefs, which represent Yin and Yang.

Among the details to look out for are the lion door guards, symbolising strength and dignity. On the right is usually a male lion pawing a ball thought to represent the world. On the left, you often find a female with a cub under her paw. At the corners of most roofs are a parade of creatures often led by a man riding a hen. These were believed to discourage lightning from striking.

Shades of Meaning

Colours and multiples also have special significance. The yellow of the palace roof stands for the Earth; red walls represents fire, luck and happiness; blue and green mean spring and rebirth. Nine is a lucky number, reflected in the number of dragons on ramps and gold studs on doors.

Approaching from **Meridian Gate** (Wumen) are the three great halls and courtyards of the outer area. The **Hall of Supreme Harmony** (Taihedian), the largest building in the palace, is the first and most impressive of these.

In its centre is the ornately carved golden Dragon Throne, from which the emperor ruled. Solemn ceremonies, such as the enthronement of a new emperor, were held here. The courtyard could hold 90,000 spectators. Behind the Hall of Supreme Harmony are the **Hall of Middle Harmony** (Zhonghedian) and the **Hall of Preserving Harmony** (Baohedian), completing a trinity reflecting the Three Buddhas and the Three Pure Ones of Taoism. To the east of the Hall of Preserving Harmony is the magnificent **Nine Dragon Screen** (Jiulongbi).

Facing the Nine Dragon Screen is the **Palace of Peace and Longevity** (Ningshougong). Puyi lived in the palace until 1925, despite the founding of the republic in 1911. In 1932, he became the puppet emperor of Manchuria, the Japanese name for their occupied territory in northeast China. Many palace treasures were stolen by the Japanese or taken to Taiwan

Left: inside the Imperial Palace. **Above:** detail of roofs and eaves
Right: the Palace of Heavenly Purity

by fleeing Nationalists, but the smaller halls to the east and west of the main halls still contain the impressive collections of the Imperial Palace. A highlight is the clock and jewellery hall, with water clocks and richly decorated mechanical clocks.

Emperors and Eunuchs

On the other side of the imposing Outer Court, to the north and separated from it by the **Gate of Heavenly Purity** (Qianqingmen), lies a labyrinth of gates, doors, pavilions, gardens and palaces. This is called the **Palace of Heavenly Purity** (Qianqinggong), the residence of the imperial family, who were almost all exclusively female; the emperor and eunuchs were the only men permitted to enter.

After dropping off your cassette player near the **Gate of Divine Warrior** (Shenwumen), the north gate of the Imperial Palace, leave by Jingshanqian Jie, a street lined with food vendors. Try a Xinjiang-style mutton kebab and take a rest, before crossing to **Jingshan Park** (Coal Hill Park; open daily 7am–7pm; entrance fee). This is the best place to appreciate the sheer scale of the palace complex. The artificial hill was built with the earth dug from the palace moats in the early 15th century. In Qing Emperor Qianlong's day, the park was stocked with deer, hares, rabbits and thousands of songbirds. The last Ming emperor, Chongzheng, fled the besieged Imperial Palace and hung himself from a tree on Jingshan in 1644. A new tree has been planted on the same spot to record the event for posterity.

If you want an early dinner, try **Dasanyuan** restaurant (open daily 7am–8.30pm; tel: 10-6401 3920) which serves good Cantonese food. Turn right as you leave Coal Hill and walk 200m (220yds) to the corner to get there or see the *Eating Out* chapter for more restaurant options.

Above: view across the city from Jingshan Park

2. FRAGRANT HILLS PARK AND THE SUMMER PALACE
(see maps, below and p31)

Visit the peaceful Fragrant Hills Park and the Summer Palace in north-west Beijing, where emperors and poets retreated from the summer heat. Stop by the Sackler Gallery on your return. The tour takes a full nine hours.

The Fragrant Hills lie 28km (18 miles) northwest of the city. Allow one hour for a taxi ride from central Beijing. Or you can take bus No 7, 15, 19, 27, 45, 102, 103 or 808 from your hotel, connecting with bus No 360 at Beijing Zoo. This would take at least 90 minutes from the city centre, followed by a 15-minute walk from the bus terminus to the park entrance.

From the 12th century to the 18th century, **Fragrant Hills Park** (Xiangshan Gongyuan; open daily 8am–5pm; in summer 8am–sunset; entrance fee) was a favourite hunting retreat for the emperors, many of whom made their mark by building pagodas and temples here. At the height of its popularity, under the Qing emperor Qianlong, the walled park was full of exotic deer. Mao Zedong lived here briefly in 1949, at Shuangqing Villa, before moving to Zhongnanhai in Beijing's west. Much of the park fell into decay or was destroyed by European troops between 1860 and 1900, but it has since been restored and is now one of the most popular destinations for day-trippers from Beijing, particularly in the autumn.

Temple Walk

This walk involves some hilly, but not difficult, terrain, so wear strong shoes and get an early start. And if the weather permits, this would be a good opportunity for a picnic lunch. The ticket office is just left of the main entrance. Once inside, follow the stone path that veers right and buy another ticket to visit the Buddhist **Temple of the Azure Clouds** (Biyunsi; open daily 8am–4pm; entrance fee).

Fragrant Hills

400 m / 440 yds

- - - - Itinerary 2

Jingangbaozuota (Diamond Throne Pagoda)
Biyunsi (Temple of the Azure Clouds)
Sun Yat-sen Memorial Hall
Hall of 500 Luohan
Cable Car Ticket Office
Beimen (North Gate)
XIANGSHAN GONGYUAN (FRAGRANT HILLS PARK)
Jianxinhai (Chamber of Introspection)
Yanjinghu (Spectacles Lake)
Cable Car
Yuhua (Fourth Jade Flower Villa)
Liulita (Glazed Tile Pagoda)
Zhaomiao (Temple of Clarity)
Xishan Qingxue (Western Hills Shimmering in Snow)
Zhao Miao (Temple of Brilliance)
Yuhua (Third Jade Flower Villa)
Xiangshan (Incense-Burner Peak)
Pavilion of Varied Scenery
Dongmen (East Gate)
Chaoyang (Sun-Facing Cave)
Qiyue (Moonlight Villa)
Lofty Phoenix Pavilion
Yuhua Shanzhuang (Jade Flower Villa)
Xiangshan Fandian (Fragrant Hills Hotel)
Senyuhu (Tree-covered Imperial Audience Tablet, Jade Sceptre Cliff)
Hongguang (Temple of Red Glow)
Banshanting (Pavilion halfway up the hill)
Jingcuiliu (Jingcui Lake)
Yuxiang (Jade Fragrance Hall)
Hillside Pavilion
White Pine Pavilion
Red-Leaf Grove
Xiangshansi (Fragrant Hills Temple)
Shuangqing Shanzhuang (Twin Pools Villa)
Beijing

A temple was first built here in 1330 and later generations added new buildings, especially during the Qing dynasty. The first hall contains two huge celestial guardians, and the second a statue of the Maitreya Buddha, all from the Ming dynasty. The innermost hall is the **Sun Yat-sen Memorial Hall**, in memory of the leader of the Nationalist movement that overthrew the Qing dynasty. To the right of his statue is a crystal coffin, a rather macabre gift from the Soviet Union.

One of the temple's more unusual treasures is the Indian-style 35m (115ft) **Diamond Throne Pagoda** at the rear of the complex. On the first level is a sanctuary with carved monster heads. This held Sun Yat-sen's body from 1925 to 1929, before it was moved to Nanjing. Climb up the inner stairs to the top terrace, with its central tower surrounded by six small pagodas covered in delicately carved *bodhisattva* (enlightened beings).

After descending and passing the Sun Yat-sen Memorial Hall, on your right you'll find the impressive **Hall of 500 Luohan**. Enter through the side gate in the lower terrace of this courtyard. The gilded wood statues (508 in all) represent legendary senior monks *(luohan)* who had achieved a higher insight into Buddhist truth and moral duty. Some of the statues meditate peacefully, one has a lion springing from his chest, while that of an old monk tears off his skin to reveal the face of a young man.

Park Peak

Walk down the hill from Biyunsi the way you came but turn right into Fragrant Hills Park proper just before you reach the exit. Another name for Fragrant Hills is **Incense Burner Peak**, a description of its appearance when fog settles on the 557m (1,827ft) summit. About 50m (55yds) along the path on the right is the ticket office for the chair lift (open daily 9am–4pm), substituting a 15-minute ride for an hour's steep climb. On the right you'll see the Diamond Throne Pagoda again, to the left is **Spectacles Lake** (Yanjinghu), named for its resemblance to a pair of spectacles, and beyond is the white glow of the luxurious Fragrant Hills Hotel.

After admiring the view from the pavilion on the summit, you have two choices. You can take the chair lift back to the bottom and head southward, visiting Spectacles Lake and the **Temple of Clarity** (Zhaomiao). Pass the east gate (but do not exit), walk several hundred metres along a leafy path that exits onto the main road leading to the Fragrant Hills Hotel. Turn right and walk 150m (165yds) to the hotel's main entrance.

If you have more energy, the path down from Incense Burner Peak starts

at the end of the pavilion furthest from the chair lift terminus. The pleasant, and not particularly demanding path, zigzags its way through lush forest. On the way down – the walk takes about 40 minutes – stay right whenever the path forks. Halfway down you'll pass an old hunting lodge, two more pavilions and the ruins of the **Fragrant Hills Temple** (Xiangshansi), in the clutches of some gnarled pines.

Just beyond the temple, the path joins a road. Turn left and walk 100m (110yds) to the main gate of the **Fragrant Hills Hotel** (Xiangshan Fandian; tel: 10-6259 1166). This oasis of luxury, designed by Chinese-American architect I M Pei, embraces classical Chinese themes such as terraces, gates within gates and court-

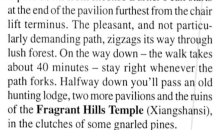

Left: gilded statues, Pavilion of 500 Luohan
Top right: the Summer Palace

yards surrounded by halls, with modern angles and skylights. In the expansive grounds, an elaborately crafted Chinese garden blends into the wooded surroundings. The architecture is inspiring but the hotel itself is rather shabby and run-down.

The hotel makes a convenient stop-off point for lunch before you take a taxi to the Summer Palace, about 10km (6 miles) away. The Western restaurant situated on the first floor and the Chinese restaurant situated on the second floor both serve good food at reasonable prices.

The Summer Palace

The **Summer Palace** (Yiheyuan; open daily, summer 6.30am–6pm, winter 8.30am–5pm; entrance fee) was built in the late Qing dynasty to replace the nearby old Summer Palace (Yuanmingyuan), which was destroyed by European allies in 1860 during the Second Opium War. The notoriously erratic Empress Dowager Cixi fulfilled a wonderful but expensive dream in 1888 when she created this sprawling playground – using 30 million taels of silver that was originally intended for the building of a naval fleet.

Originally a concubine of the third rank, Cixi had placed herself on the Dragon Throne after the death of the emperor Xianfeng in 1861, and ruled unscrupulously for the next 50 years in the name of her young child. In 1900, a large part of the palace was destroyed by the Europeans when the Boxer rebels laid siege to foreigners in Beijing.

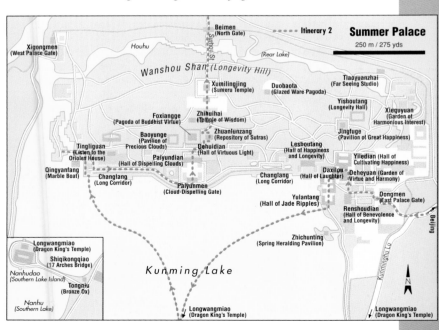

As in every classical Chinese garden, water and mountains (usually represented by rocks) determine the landscape of the Summer Palace. The grounds cover more than 30sq km (10sq miles), three-quarters of which is occupied by **Kunming Lake**; but the following route takes in the highlights without wearing out your shoes. Inside the main gate, the lavishly furnished **Hall of Benevolence and Longevity** (Renshoudian) was where Cixi held audiences with ministers and handled other state business in the summer months. Behind it, veer right to the **Garden of Virtue and Harmony** (Deheyuan), with a three-storey open-air theatre at the centre. Here, Cixi used to enjoy operatic performances by her 384-strong ensemble of eunuchs. Using a system of trap doors between the stages, the eunuchs' elaborate productions featured immortals falling from the sky and evil spirits rising from the depths. The refurbished **Hall of Laughter** (Daxilou) opposite the theatre is where Cixi and her court sat to view the performances. The halls on the periphery of the court house many royal objects.

Taking the Dragon Boat

Backtrack to the **Hall of Jade Ripples** (Yulantang), on the edge of the lake, where you can buy a ticket for a tour by the 'dragon boat'. From the boat you can see the **Bridge of Seventeen Arches** (Shiqikongqiao) and the **Dragon King's Temple** (Longwangmiao) on a small island. The boat lands at the **Longevity Hill** (Wanshou Shan), where 150m (164yds) along the shore stands the famous **Marble Boat** (Qingyanfang), a folly in which Cixi once took tea.

If you don't feel up to a steep climb over the Hill of Longevity, continue in the same direction around the back of the hill, following signposts to the

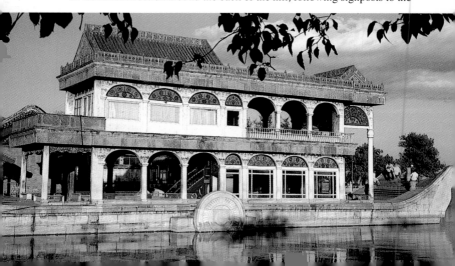

shopper's paradise of Suzhou Street. Or walk back to the boat launch area to start an amble down the **Long Corridor** (Changlang). It runs for 700m (765yds) parallel to the northern shore of the lake, linking the scattered palace buildings. The light wooden construction is decorated with countless scenes from ancient Chinese mythology.

Halfway along the Long Corridor you'll come to a *pailou*, a triumphal arch, where you begin your ascent to the imposing Buddhist temple complex on the top of the hill. The **Hall of Dispelling Clouds** (Paiyundian) is where the Empress Cixi celebrated her birthdays, and some of her presents are displayed there. Beyond is the **Hall of Virtuous Light** (Dehuidian) and, up the winding stone stairs, the massive octagonal **Temple of Buddhist Virtue** (Foxiangge).

Adjacent, on the west side, is one of the few buildings that survived the destruction of 1900 undamaged, the **Pavilion of Precious Clouds** (Baoyunge). Though it looks wooden, its beams, columns and roof struts are made of cast bronze. The final short climb takes you to the **Temple of Wisdom** (Zhihuihai), at the top of Longevity Hill. Built in 1750, it is covered with countless ceramic Buddhas. Many of the lower Buddhas were either smashed or beheaded by Red Guards during the Cultural Revolution.

Shopping on Suzhou Street

Just behind the Temple of Wisdom, follow the upper path on the right side and then descend among the square towers and stupas of the **Sumeru Temple** (Xumilingjing) on your left. At its base, you'll find your final reward in the Summer Palace, **Suzhou Street**. The street was created as a replica of a 19th-century canal-side shopping area in Suzhou, to allow Cixi and her court to enjoy the pleasures of shopping without having to mix with ordinary mortals. It was restored in 1990 and you, too, can enjoy a peaceful stroll through little speciality shops run by assistants in period costume. Browse for kites, ceramics and calligraphy and stop at a teahouse. Leave the Summer Palace on the north side of Suzhou Street.

If you have time on the way back to the city, visit the **Sackler Gallery** (open daily 9am–5pm; entrance fee) on Beijing University's campus. Enter by the west gate of the university. The gallery is the second building on the left after the bridge. View artefacts spanning 280,000 years, which for seven decades were stacked in the university's archaeology department. The display is well designed and the museum not too large, so you can pass from Paleolithic humanoids to the Qing dynasty in a matter of 45 minutes.

Top left: bridge over the western part of Kunming Lake
Left: Cixi's Marble Boat. **Above:** the Long Corridor

beijing & environs

3. TEMPLE OF HEAVEN AND THE
NATURAL HISTORY MUSEUM *(see map, below)*

Early morning exercise rituals in the Temple of Heaven park, followed by an exploration of the temple complex, a stop at the Natural History Museum and shopping at Hongqiao Market. This is a half-day tour.

Take a taxi or bus No 106, 6, 34, 35 or 36 to the north gate of the Temple of Heaven Park.

Enclosed by a wall 5km (3 miles) long, the **Temple of Heaven** (Tiantan; park open daily 6am–8pm; temple open daily 8am–5pm; park entrance fee includes temple) is the best place in Beijing to catch a glimpse of some traditional, and some not so traditional, forms of Chinese culture. Along the paths or among the trees, *qigong* practitioners strengthen their internal systems through concentration and slow-motion exercises that stimulate breathing and circulation. Plan to arrive by 7am if you want to see early-morning enthusiasts of *qigong*, *taiqi*, calligraphy, Peking opera and kite-flying. The temple complex was originally constructed between 1406 and 1429 under Emperor Yongle of the Ming dynasty. It was used for imperial sacrifices just twice a year: at the winter solstice, when the emperor thanked the gods for the last harvest; and on the 15th day of the first month of the lunar year (Lantern Festival), when he begged the gods to bless the coming harvest.

The Hall of Prayer for Good Harvests

The park is round in the north, representing Heaven, and square in the south, representing Earth. Find your way through it to the city's most elegant and possibly most recognised structure, the **Hall of Prayer for Good Harvests** (Qi'niandian). An exquisite example of Chinese wooden buildings, constructed without the use of a single nail, the round hall is 40m (130ft) high. Its three levels are covered with deep blue tiles symbolising the colour of heaven. The roof is supported by 28 pillars: the four largest ones, in the centre, represent the four seasons; the double ring of 12 pillars represents the 12 months, as well as the traditional divisions of the Chinese day, each comprising two hours. Intricate carpentry creates the dome high overhead; below are thrones where tablets commemorating the ancestors were placed. Destroyed several times, the hall was faithfully rebuilt in 1890.

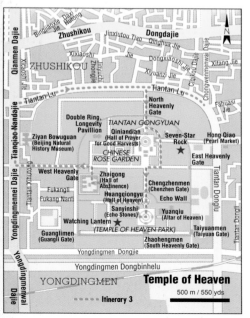

Temple of Heaven

500 m / 550 yds

Itinerary 3

Above: roof detail, Temple of Heaven
Right: the Imperial Vault of Heaven

Head south to the **Imperial Vault of Heaven** (Huangqiongyu), much smaller but with similar deep blue roof tiles representing Heaven. The ancestral tablets were stored here until needed for the prayer ceremony. It is now best known for its acoustics. Stand on the first of the three **Echo Stones** (Sanyinshi), in front of the entrance, and clap; you will hear a single echo. Do the same on the second stone and you'll hear a double echo; and on the third, a triple echo. Whisper into the **Echo Wall**, enclosing the courtyard around the hall, and the other person will be able to hear every word anywhere along the wall. Walk south to the **Altar of Heaven** (Yuanqiu) where three concentric terraces stand inside two enclosures – one square (Earth) and one round (Heaven). Animal sacrifices took place inside the square enclosure while the emperor prayed at the centre of the mound.

Palaces, Museums and Markets

On the way to the west exit of the temple, you'll pass through the courtyard of the **Hall of Abstinence** (Zhaigong). The hall has a double moat spanned by a series of fine stone bridges, and its courtyard has a beautiful drum and bell tower. Twice a year, the emperor would spend a night of fasting and celibacy in the palace prior to the sacrificial rites the next morning. These rituals, which survived until 1914, go back 4,000 years. Leave by the west gate, just north of the Palace of Abstinence. Outside the gate, you'll run into the main north–south street, Tianqiao Nandajie, after walking about 100m (110yds). Turn right and walk about 300m (330yds) to the **Natural History Museum** (Ziran Bowuguan; open daily 8.30am–5pm; entrance fee), filled with many interesting and some bizarre exhibits.

A five-minute taxi ride will take you to the northeast corner of the park where, across the street, is **Hongqiao Market** (Hongqiao Shichang; open daily 8.30am–7pm). Built in 1995 to replace the old market that used to hug the park's wall, the new indoor market has everything from meat, fish and spices to toys, clothes and antiques. For lunch, backtrack 400m (436yds) to the north gate of the Temple of Heaven. Across Tiantan Road you'll see **Yushan Restaurant** (87 Tiantan Lu; open daily 10.30am–1.30pm, 4.30pm–8pm; tel: 10-6701 4263) which specialises in Manchu-Han imperial banquets. Try the sesame cake with minced pork filling – the Chinese version of the hamburger.

4. Marco Polo Bridge, Niujie Mosque and Fayuansi Temple *(see map, p18–19)*

The highlights of southwest Beijing, beginning with the Marco Polo Bridge in the suburbs of Wanping, and then a visit to two working religious centres. This is a half-day tour.

Take a mini-van or taxi to Wanping, 15km (9 miles) southwest of Beijing. Ask the driver to wait or you may have a gruelling trip back on bus No 339.

In the 13th century, the Venetian merchant Marco Polo was on his way back to the West as an emissary of Kublai Khan when he encountered **Lugouqiao**, a stone bridge spanning the Yongding River. He gave it such rave reviews that Europeans dubbed it the **Marco Polo Bridge**. The bridge was built in 1189 during the Jin dynasty and rebuilt in the same style in 1698 after being badly damaged by a flood. Each of its 140 stone columns is topped with an ornately carved lion. Emperor Qianlong added to the bridge's fame when he wrote the poem *Morning Moon over Lugou Bridge* in 1751.

The 'Marco Polo Bridge' Incident

You can see the emperor's poetry, in his own calligraphy, engraved on steles next to the bridge. The bridge was one of the main routes into the capital for camel trains and was used by motor traffic until the 1980s.

In Marco Polo's day, **Wanping** was a busy little riverside town full of inns and restaurants used by merchants. Under a grand scheme announced several years ago by the government, the old town was to be recreated, with facilities like a horse track, paddle boats and Qing-style homes. The city wall and gate towers were completed, but the money ran out.

The bridge is also famous for the July 1937 'Marco Polo Bridge Incident,' which marked China's entry into World War II. Japanese troops, who had seized control of a railway junction near Wanping, were fired on by Chinese soldiers.

Above and left: Marco Polo Bridge

The Japanese, who already occupied northeast China and Taiwan, used the incident as a pretext for a full-scale invasion of Beijing and most of China. In the centre of Wanping, about 10 minutes walk into town along the main street, is the **Memorial Hall of the War of Resistance Against Japan** (Zhonggui Remin Kangri Zhanzheng Jinian Guan Bowuguan; open daily 8am–4pm; entrance fee). It contains an interesting pictorial history of the war from the Chinese perspective.

Get your driver to drop you at **Niujie Mosque** (Niujie Qingzhensi; open daily 8am–4pm; entrance fee), also known as Ox Street Mosque. Built in AD996 in Arabic style, it has all the features of mosques elsewhere in the world – minaret, prayer hall facing Mecca and Arabic inscriptions – but in distinctly Chinese-style buildings. Islam reached China during the Tang dynasty (AD618–907) via Arab merchants. Muslims now live in all parts of the country. This mosque is the oldest and largest of about 50 mosques in Beijing.

Prayer takes place five times a day in the main prayer hall. There is a separate women's hall. Geometric designs and Arabic script adorn the walls inside, as the Koran allows no graven images, animal or human. The mosque is an active place of worship and a gathering place for Beijing's Muslim community, numbering about 180,000. Female visitors need not cover their heads to enter, but shorts or short skirts are not allowed (the caretaker can lend you a pair of baggy pants) and non-Muslims cannot enter the prayer hall.

Temple of Buddhist Doctrine

To get to the **Temple of the Source of Buddhist Doctrine** (Fayuansi), take a 15- to 20-minute walk through the *hutong* (alleys). Turn right on Ox Street (Nin Jie) as you leave the mosque. About 100m (110yds) along, turn right again into Shuru Hutong, which has a Chinese archway at its entrance. It's easy to spot where the wealthy lived: doors to better courtyard homes are marked with more elaborate *mendui* – two carved stones placed on either side of the door. Walk along the *hutong* for about 500m (545yds). Midway, you'll cross a wide *hutong* identifiable by a public toilet at the corner. At the end of Shuru, turn right onto Xizhuan Hutong. Walk about 400m (436yds) and take a right into Fayuansi Qianhutong. The temple gate is just 50m (55yds) after the turn.

The Temple of the Source of Buddhist Doctrine (open daily 8.30am–4pm, closed Wed; entrance fee), is one of the oldest surviving and most pleasant Buddhist temples in Beijing. It was built in AD645 and was formerly called Temple of the Loyal (Minzhongsi), to honour soldiers killed in battle. Today, it houses the Buddhist Academy, formed in 1956, devoted to training Buddhist novices who are then sent to monasteries across China. The academy has a library of more than 100,000 precious texts and an exhibition of Buddhist sculpture, some dating from the Han dynasty. Inside some of the temple halls are fine bronzes, some Ming dynasty, and a 6-m (20-ft) sleeping Buddha.

Right: roof detail at Niujie Mosque

5. BEIJING HOTEL AND THE FOREIGN LEGATION QUARTER *(see map, p39)*

Breakfast at the Beijing Hotel followed by an architectural tour of early 20th-century Beijing through the former Foreign Legation Quarter. This route can either be done on foot (approx 2hrs), or by bike. Bicycles can be rented from the bicycle park at the east end of the Beijing Hotel.

Take bus No 1, 4, 52, 57, 37, 10, 20 or 120 to Tiananmen Square and walk east one block to Beijing Hotel on Dongchang'an Jie.

The gargantuan **Beijing Hotel** (33 Dongchang'an Jie; tel: 10-6513 7766) was built during four different eras, and the spirit of each is reflected in the hotel's various sections. Start at the eastern end. Bleak, square and utilitarian, this wing was built in 1974 as the Cultural Revolution was reaching its climax, two years before Mao's death. Next is the oldest remaining section. Built in 1917, the ornate French-style vaulted ceilings, arched windows and stairway sweeping up through the centre evoke images of the decadent 1920s. The French-style café in this section (open daily 6.30am–midnight) is a nice and quiet spot for morning coffee. Beyond is the extension built in 1954, reflecting the optimism following Communist victory. It has a Chinese-style bracketed ceiling and a lavish banquet hall where foreign government officials were once entertained. The westernmost section, the Grand Hotel, is an eclectic 1989 addition and a tribute to the new money of the reform era.

European Legacy

Early 20th century European architecture in China is an instant reminder of the ignominious decline of the Qing dynasty and the foreign domination that followed. The **Foreign Legation Quarter**, south of the Beijing Hotel and east of Tiananmen Square, contains many elegant European buildings that recall part of modern China's history. Between the 1860s and the outbreak of the Sino-Japanese War in 1937, 13 foreign governments were represented here, their presence forced on the Chinese by the outcome of the

Above: the coffee shop in the Beijing Hotel

Opium Wars. They had their own administration, police, churches, hospitals, shops and post office, guarded by some 1,000 soldiers. After 1900, when the Boxers launched a 45-day attack here, the area was closed off to Chinese nationals.

To get there, leave Beijing Hotel at its east end and head south across Dongchang'an Jie and down Taijichang Dajie (Customs Street). About 200m (220yds) along on the right, you'll come to the gate of the former **Italian Legation**, where the Italians relocated in 1900 after the Boxer rebels destroyed their previous quarters. It now houses the **Chinese People's Association for Friendship with Foreign Countries** (CPAFFC).

House of Many Owners

Continue along Taijichang Dajie but cross to the opposite side. Walk alongside a high gray wall topped with curved tiles and turn left into the first alleyway. About 200m (220yds) on the left is the gate to the former **Hungaria Legation**, now the **Institute of International Studies**. Built in 1900, the simple grey and white building has changed hands many times. In 1915, when China declared war on Germany and its allies, the building was occupied by the Hungarians. After a short spell under the Dutch, a Russian general turned it into a guesthouse in the late 1920s. In 1938, it became the German Club. The Americans used it for Allied Property Administration and it later became the Hungarian Embassy. The building was finally returned to the Chinese in 1969.

Double back to Taijichang Dajie and turn left. Through the first gate on the left is an elegant grey-blue building with arches along the ground floor, topped by a red national emblem and a single portal. This is the headquarters of the **Beijing People's Congress** (no entry to the public). Built in 1902, it was once the **Peking Club**, with a swimming pool and tennis courts

beijing & environs

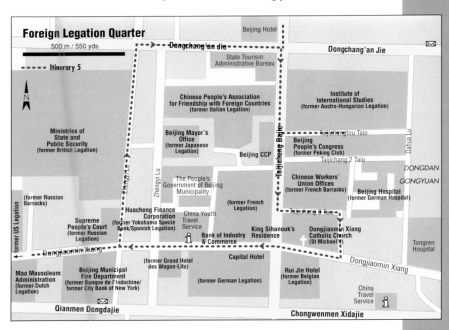

Foreign Legation Quarter

500 m / 550 yds

- - - - Itinerary 5

N

Beijing Hotel

Dongchang'an Jie   Dongchang'an Jie

State Tourism
Administrative Bureau

Chinese People's Association
for Friendship with Foreign Countries
(former Italian Legation)

Institute of
International Studies
(former Austro-Hungarian Legation)

Ministries of
State and
Public Security
(former British Legation)

Beijing Mayor's
Office
(former Japanese
Legation)

Beijing CCP

Taijichang Dajie

Taijichangtou Taio

Beijing
People's Congress
(former Peking Club)

Taijichang 2 Taio

Datua Lu

DONGDAN

The People's
Government of Beijing
Municipality

Zhengyi Lu

Chinese Workers'
Union Offices
(former French Barracks)

DONGGUAN

Beijing Hospital
(former German Hospital)

(former Russian
Barracks)

(former French
Legation)

Taijichang 3 Taio

(former US Legation)

Supreme
People's Court
(former Russian
Legation)

Huacheng Finance
Corporation
(former Yokohama Specie
Bank/Spanish Legation)

China Youth
Travel
Service

Bank of Industry
& Commerce

King Sihanouk's
Residence

Dongjiaomin Xiang
Catholic Church
(St Michael's)

Tongren
Hospital

Dongjiaomin Xiang

Capital Hotel

Dongjiaomin Xiang

Mao Mausoleum
Administration
(former Dutch
Legation)

Beijing Municipal
Fire Department
(former Banque de l'Indochine/
former City Bank of New York)

(former Grand Hotel
des Wagon-Lits)

(former German Legation)

Rui Jin Hotel
(former Belgian
Legation)

China
Travel
Service

Qianmen Dongdajie

Chongwenmen Xidajie

that were still in use as late as the 1960s. The white building opposite, topped with an enormous red star, is the headquarters for the Beijing municipality Communist Party Committee.

Moving along Taijichang Dajie, you'll enter 'Little France'. The French, along with the British, were the first to install permanent diplomatic representatives here. They held large tracts of land on both sides of the street. On the right side of the street are the graceful roof lines of the former **French Legation**. Turn left at the second alleyway, about 200m (220yds) beyond the Peking Club. French theologian Teilhard de Chardin, who lived in China from 1932 to 1946, founded an institute of geobiology on this street. Much of this area has been replaced with typical Chinese apartment blocks, but about 100m (110yds) along on the left, you can peer through the gates of the former **French Barracks**. The Soviet-style building at the centre is now the **Chinese Workers' Union** offices.

Continue another 100m (110yds) along this alleyway and turn right. After another 100m (110yds), you will reach **Dongjiaomin Xiang** (Legation Street). Turn right again. Just before the next junction, about 200m (220yds) along on the right, is **St Michael's Church**, an intimate little neo-Gothic church built by the French Vincentian Order in 1902. St Michael's was closed after the 1949 revolution, but was renovated and reopened in 1989. During the week, you can enter the chapel from a door on the right side but do try and keep quiet as there are usually people worshipping. The figures of the saints above the chapel doors date all the way back to 1889 and some of the stained glass and ceramic tiles are original too.

More Overseas Legations

Opposite the church, you can see the jagged brick roof lines and green tops of the former **Belgian Legation**. Before 1900, this was the home of a high level Chinese official, Xu Tong, who hated foreigners so much that he purportedly wished to cover his sedan chair with their skin. He did his best to avoid the barbarians, but when the Allied armies entered Beijing in 1900 in reaction to the Boxer Rebellion, Xu Tong could take it no longer. He committed suicide.

From St Michael's, cross Taijichang Dajie and continue along Dongjiaomin Xiang. About 50m (55yds) past the junction, where two massive stone lions and two armed soldiers stand guard, are the red gates of another building belonging to the former **French Legation**. This is now the occasional residence of Cambodian King Norodom Sihanouk, a favour from the Chinese government when he went into exile. Across the road is the gate to the former offices of Jardine Matheson, one of the earliest and most aggressive Western trading companies in Asia.

Left: St Michael's Church

About 200m (220yds) further along Dongjiaomin Xiang, you'll pass a tiny building on the right with fancy brickwork, a zigzag roof line and arched windows. This is a branch of the **Bank of Industry and Commerce**. Until recently, it was a post office and was also the site of the original Beijing Hotel before it moved to its current location in 1900.

Next to it is the beginning of the former **Spanish Legation** (which used to extend all the way to the corner), where the protocol on the Boxer Rebellion was signed in 1901. The Spanish sold the corner lot to the Yokohama Specie Bank, now the **Huacheng Finance Corporation**. Empress Dowager Cixi was said to have borrowed money here just before the last dynasty fell. The valuables she put up as collateral were never reclaimed and are now in a collection in London. The Huacheng Finance Corporation stands on the corner of Dongjiaomin Xiang and Zhengyi Lu, the divided north-south street. Zhengyi means 'justice', but the road used to be called Canal Street because there was a trench that carried sewage water. It was filled in 1925 to create the promenade between the two lanes.

Cross Zhengyi Lu and continue on Dongjiaomin Xiang. On the right, behind the row of fruit vendors, is the site of the Russian Orthodox Mission, which later became the **Russian Legation** and then the Soviet Legation. Until 1991, there was a simple stone building here, probably the former Russian church. Now there is a shiny white building housing the **Supreme Court**. About 300m (330yds) further down on the left side of the street, you will find a brick structure with a green roof. The building was formerly the **Dutch Legation**, and is now the office of the **Mao Mausoleum Administration**.

The British Legation

Retrace your steps along Dongjiaomin Xiang and turn left on Zhengyi Lu for the final stretch. The area on the right side of Zhengyi Lu, north of the Huacheng Finance Corporation, was the **Japanese Legation**. It now houses the **Beijing Mayor's Office** and the offices of the city government.

The last, and possibly grandest relic on this walk is further along Zhengyi Lu on the left: the former **British Legation**. The British moved in after the Second Opium War of 1860 and expanded the area to create the largest territory held by foreigners. They kept this compound until 1959, but it is now occupied by the **Ministries of State and Public Security**, the Chinese version of the KGB.

The Legation loop brings you to the corner of Zhengyi Lu and Dongchang'an Jie, across from the Beijing Hotel.

Above: Huacheng Finance Corporation
Right: former Japanese Legation

beijing & environs

6. LAMA TEMPLE, CONFUCIUS TEMPLE AND DITAN PARK
(see map, p18–19)

An introduction to two different Chinese philosophical traditions, followed by dinner and dancing at Ditan Park. The three sites are all within a 1-km (½-mile) radius so the tour is an easy walk or bicycle ride.

Take the subway to Yonghegong station (under the temple). After leaving the station, turn left onto Yonghegong Dajie. The main gate of the Lama Temple (Yonghegong) is 100m (110yds) along on the left.

Buddhism came to China from India as early as the 1st century, but Lamaism, the mystical sect of Tibetan Buddhism that incorporates shamanist beliefs and practices, only gained influence in the eastern part of China after the Mongols conquered Tibet and China in the 13th century. The Manchus practised Lamaism, so its influence revived under the Qing dynasty.

The Lama Temple

Originally the private residence of Prince Yong, the **Lama Temple** (Yonghegong; open daily 9am–4pm; entrance fee), was turned into a monastery after its owner became Emperor Yongzheng in 1723. According to ancient Chinese custom, the former residence of a Son of Heaven had to be dedicated to religious purposes once he left. Therefore, in 1744, Yongzheng's son, Emperor Qianlong, established it as a Lamaist monastery, and it soon flourished as a centre of Lamaist religion and art. At the same time, the monastery offered the Qing rulers welcome opportunities for influencing and controlling Tibetan and Mongolian subjects. It remained a monastery until 1960.

The temple, the most elaborately restored sacred building in Beijing, belongs to the Yellow Hat sect, whose spiritual leader is the Dalai Lama. Since the Chinese invasion of Tibet in 1950, relations between the authorities and Buddhist leaders have been problematic. The current Dalai Lama fled to India in 1959 after failing to win independence for Tibet. He is still condemned by Beijing, but his image, once forbidden, can now be displayed in temples. The government officially remains atheist, but during the reforms

since 1978, temples and churches have been restored, along with the right to worship.

The Lama Temple has five halls and three gates laid out along a north–south axis. In each successive hall, the central Buddha is more imposing than the last; in the three-storied section of the fifth hall, **Pavilion of Ten Thousand Happinesses** (Wanfuge) is a 23-m (75-ft) statue of the Buddha carved from a single piece of sandalwood. Today, about 70 monks live here (if you want to photograph them, first make sure they don't mind). No photos are allowed inside.

Lamaism seems benign and introspective, but its roots lie in the dark and mysterious rituals of the ancient Tibetan Bön religion. Take a close look at the carvings and Tibetan *thangka* paintings in the side halls. One image shows the goddess Lamo riding a horse cloaked in the skin of her own son, sacrificed to show her detachment from the world.

The Temple of Confucius

Next stop is a tranquil former centre of scholarship, the **Confucius Temple** (Kong Miao; open Tues–Sat 8.30–5pm; entrance fee). Go west on Guozijian Jie, the street opposite the Lama Temple across Yonghegong Dajie. The entrance to the Confucius Temple is 200m (220yds) on the right.

In its glorious past, emperors came to offer sacrifices to Confucius at the Hall of Great Achievement, hoping for guidance in ruling. Confucius was a teacher in the state of Lu (in present day Shandong province) in the 6th century BC, about the same time as Buddha was teaching in India. The brand of Confucianism adopted by the emperors stressed order, and so, Confucianism was an important tool for keeping order across the vast and diverse nation. It teaches that if a ruler is moral and follows the proper rites and rituals, his subjects will fall in line. The same applies to husbands and wives, masters and servants, parents and children.

Built in 1306 during the Yuan dynasty, this is the second-largest Confucian temple in China, after the one in Confucius' hometown, Qufu. The temple's prize possession is a collection of 190 steles (upright stone tablets) inscribed with records of ancient civil service examinations, which are housed in the first of the four courtyards.

Leave the temple, turn right and walk 200m (220yds) along Guozijian Jie for a brief look at the former **Imperial Academy** (Guozijian; open daily 8.30am–5pm; entrance fee), now the Capital Library. Once the highest educational institution in the land, thousands of students and scholars came here to listen to the emperor expound Confucian classics. A set of steles commissioned by Emperor Qianlong records 13 Confucian classics. The 800,000 characters were engraved by a single scholar over 12 years.

Left: Lama Temple, Gate of Honour **Above:** Confucius Temple pavilion
Right: Confucius Temple stone stele

By this time, you'll be ready for earthly pleasures: food, song and dance. Proceed to **Ditan Park** (Ditan Gongyuan; open daily 6am–9pm; entrance fee) by returning to Yonghegong Jie and walking north across the Second Ring Road. The entrance to the park is 300m (330yds) north of the Yonghegong subway station, to the left. Ditan (the Altar of the Earth), first built in 1530, had a similar ritual function as the Temple of Heaven. Each year, on the summer solstice throughout the Ming and Qing dynasties, the emperor came here to make sacrifices. The mound, a round platform surrounded by two concentric square walls where the sacrifice was offered, was restored in the 1980s.

To the west of the mound, a hall that once housed the sacred tablets, and later held weapons, has been converted into the **Fangzitan Arts and Crafts**

Store (open daily 10.30am–9pm). Around the mound to the north side is **Fengrusong Restaurant** (open daily 10.30am–2pm, 4.30–8pm), which serves good Cantonese dishes. The menu is in Chinese, but the waitresses speak some English. Check prices before ordering; dishes range from 15 to 350 yuan. After dinner, join one of the popular pastimes of modern China, ballroom dancing. A 'dance party' is held nightly (7.30–9.30pm, if weather permits, from March to mid-October) at **Lie Yuan Flower Garden**, 200m (220yds) north of the restaurant. The park officially closes at 9pm but the gate is open all night to accommodate ballroom dancers. The park also holds one of Beijing's best Spring Festival temple fairs, with performances including Peking opera, folk dancing, re-enactments of Qing dynasty imperial rituals, as well as stalls selling traditional snacks.

7. DAZHALAN AND LIULICHANG *(see map, p18–19)*

A walk through the fascinating *hutong* (alleyways) of two neighbourhoods outside Qianmen gate. Takes between 30 minutes and three hours depending on whether you stop to shop.

Take the subway to Qianmen Station and cross to the corner southwest from Tiananmen Square (by Kentucky Fried Chicken and Vie de France).

Dazhalan, extending south and west from Qianmen (Front Gate), was once synonymous with decadence and squalor. During the Ming and Qing dynasties, the district was full of theatres, teahouses, brothels and beggars. All the vulgar activities forbidden in the Imperial Palace flourished here.

If you're facing the Vie de France, turn left and then veer right, following the street as it rounds the traffic circle just south of Tiananmen Square. Walk about 100m (110yds) between two rows of densely-packed food and clothing vendors. Turn right onto **Zhubaoshi Jie** (Jewellery Street), in the heart of the market. This street runs parallel to Qianmen Dajie, its entrance marked by an enormous Phoenix Bicycles billboard.

Above: Peking opera at Lie Yuan Flower Garden

There are bargains galore here, although some products are of poor quality. With hawkers shouting prices from all sides, music blaring, and egg vendors and pedicab drivers pushing their way through the crowd, it's easy to imagine Dazhalan at the turn of the 20th century. Prostitution in Dazhalan, once a deeply entrenched feature, has all but disappeared under communism. There were various classes of brothels, and during the Nationalist period, the women were registered and given regular health checks. The economic reforms of the 1980s and 1990s have seen prostitution make a gradual, if less visible, comeback in Beijing (though not in Dazhalan) and other Chinese cities. The authorities ignore it so long as it is restricted to the usual hairdressing salons, massage parlours and hotels.

Clothing and Fabrics

About 300m (330yds) along, Zhubaoshi Jie intersects with **Dazhalan Jie**, a wide and bustling alley with a green police booth on the left side of the corner. Turn right, then 20m (22yds) along on the right you'll see a building with extravagant wrought-iron gatework in green, the **Qianmen Women's Clothing Store** (open daily 9am–8pm). If you want clothes tailored in China, check out the wide choice of fabrics on the second floor.

The same goes for the **Ruifuxiang Silk and Cotton Fabric Store** (open daily 9am–7.30pm) two doors down, with a pretentious marble entrance. Ruifuxiang was built here in 1893 by a Shandong businessman and catered to society's upper crust, including wives and concubines of the Imperial Court.

At 18 Dazhalan Xijie, return briefly to the socialist era with a visit to the **Underground City** (open daily 8am–5pm; free). The entrance is marked by a sign in English with an arrow pointing down the stairs of a clothing store to the left. In the late 1960s, at the height of China's Cold War with the Soviet Union, the Chinese feared nuclear or conventional attack and Mao Zedong ordered the rapid construction of a huge system of air-raid shelters. Now often used as shopping centres or warehouses, the shelters remain in cities across China. The whole Beijing tunnel system is believed to cover more than 30km (19 miles). The part you see at Dazhalan is just 270m (295yds) long, in some places as deep as 15m (50ft).

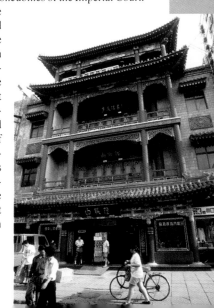

Above: Dazhalan bazaar
Right: Dazhalan Xijie store

beijing & environs

Back on the surface and still on the left side, just a few doors beyond the Underground City, at No 22 is **Zhang Yiyuan Tea Shop** (open daily 8am–8pm) with bas-relief flower designs under its windows. This is a good place to shop for your favourite tea. Next door at No 24 is the **Tongren Traditional Medicine Shop** (open daily 8am–7.30pm), once responsible for keeping secret medicinal recipes for the emperor. It's been here since 1669 and the pharmacist still weighs age-old herbal remedies with a hand-held scale. Look out for the incredible array of cures, from deer antlers and whole newts to ginseng for curing impotence and enhancing the libido.

Further down, at No 34, is an ornate and traditional Chinese-style four-storey building, the **Neiliansheng Shoe Store** (open daily 8.30am–8pm), built in 1853. There is nothing traditional about the chrome and glass interior displays with the latest shoe styles. You can be shod cheaply, but only if your feet are fairly delicate, American size 8 or smaller for women.

Communal Living

Walk 300m (330yds) along Dazhalan and you'll arrive at another junction with a little green police booth. Turn right and then, another 30m (33yds) fur-

ther, left. This is **Yangmei Alley**, a typical Beijing *hutong* with children, old people and the smells of cooking and communal toilets mingled together. Most of the doors lead into *siheyuan*, courtyards with rooms on four sides facing inwards. Life in these houses is not very comfortable. In summer, the heat drives the inhabitants out to the streets. In winter, most homes are heated by coal-burning stoves.

After another 400m (440yds), Yangmei Alley takes a little jog to the right, where you will see an antiques shop on your left. Turn left to **Liulichang**, a successfully restored section of the old city jam-packed with curios, carpets and antiques. This has been a shopping area for books and antiques for more than 300 years. In the Ming dynasty, Liulichang, which means 'glazed-tile factory', was one of the sites where tiles were made for the imperial buildings. Later, it was developed into a cultural centre for scholar-officials who stocked up on calligraphy materials, books and seals.

Check out **Rongbaozhai** (open daily 9am–5.30pm), a 17th-century shop at No 19, famous for its range of watercolour block paintings, charcoal rubbings and reproductions of old paintings.

For dinner, why not try the **Confucian Heritage Restaurant** (open daily 10.30am–1.30pm; 4.30–8pm), a cozy little teahouse at No 3 specialising in some curiously exotic Shandong dishes with tantalising names such as 'Supernatural Duck'.

Above: gallery in Liulichang

8. THE LAKE DISTRICT *(see map, p18–19)*

Explore the ancient Drum and Bell Towers and a farmers' market; walk along the lakes and dine in the imperial gardens of Beihai Park. Walk, or cycle if you prefer. This half-day tour is designed for the afternoon, but can easily be adapted for the morning.

Take a taxi to the Drum and Bell Towers. You'll spot the towers just north of the junction of Di'anmen Dajie and Gulou Dongdajie. Or you could take public bus Nos 58 or 815, or trolley bus No 107, both of which stop just 50m (55yds) from the Drum Tower.

Browse around the lively market in the old neighbourhood between the Drum Tower and the Bell Tower. You'll find live shrimps, spices, vegetables and home-made noodles in this fresh produce market filled with strange and exotic smells. The covered market at the centre is a good place to get acquainted with Beijing's snack foods: *haobing* (griddle-fried cakes with sesame seeds on top), *qiehe* (fried stuffed eggplant), *chao tianluo* (fried river snails) and *douzhi* (milky dough made from beans). Stick to hot-off-the-stove food if you don't wish to risk an upset stomach.

The Bell and Drum Towers

The grey **Bell Tower** (Zhonglou) and the red **Drum Tower** (Gulou) (both open daily 9am–4.30pm; entrance fee) are the legacy of Kublai Khan. He had the original ones built nearby to serve as the imperial clock. The Drum Tower used to hold 24 giant drums. They were beaten to mark the closing of the city gates and the passing of the night watches. The bell struck the time of day. As with most Mongol buildings, the towers were replaced in 1420 during the Ming dynasty. The Bell Tower, which was made of wood, burned down and was rebuilt of stone in 1747.

The 33m (108ft) Bell Tower is more interesting structurally. Its stone staircase leads through a dark passageway reminis-

Above: view from the Drum Tower
Right: one of the drums at the Drum Tower

cent of medieval castles. In 1990, the bell was re-installed in the tower. Since then the mayor has climbed the tower at every Spring Festival to ring in the Lunar New Year. A chief attraction of the Drum Tower is the view from the top over the surrounding area of traditional *siheyuan* courtyard houses.

In the hall at the top is one original drum, damaged during the Opium Wars, flanked by two replicas. It also houses a black-and-white photo exhibition by Xu Yong, which is part of his *101 Photographs of Beijing Hutongs* collection.

To start your walk around the lakes, go south on Di'anmen Dajie and turn right on the first alleyway you come to, about 50m (55yds) along. This narrow lane leads past a line of hairdressers and old guesthouses. Another 150m (165yds) along is a junction where you should make a left turn. Ahead is a stone bridge that divides **Houhai** (Rear Lake) from **Qianhai** (Front Lake). The two are part of a string of six lakes extending all the way from the north to the south of the old Inner City.

The Lotus Flower Market

Cross the little stone bridge and turn left on the path that runs along the shore of Qianhai. The south end of Qianhai is where the action is. About 700m (765yds) along on the southwest shore is the **Lotus Flower Market**, a great place to hang around until evening and savour Beijing snacks. Round the southwest corner of the lake is a shady area. When the weather is fine, musicians gather there with their traditional instruments and create a marvelous cacophony. The lake draws swimmers in the summer, skaters in the winter and strollers all year round.

Cross Di'anmen Xidajie and just off to the right is the north entrance to **Beihai** (North Lake Park; open daily 6.30am–8pm; entrance fee). The area around the lake served as imperial residence for every dynasty that had its capital in Beijing. At the end of the imperial era in 1925, Beihai was opened to the public. But **Zhongnanhai** (Central and Southern Lake), surrounded by a thick wall, remain the cloistered domain of the Chinese leadership.

Zhongnanhai is today the site of the Politburo and State Council offices. Also known as the 'New Forbidden City', it is closed to the public.

The focal point of the park is Jade Island (Qionghuadao), once the site of the winter residence of Kublai Khan – but first skirt the western shore to see the **Nine Dragon Screen** (Jiulongbi), one of three in the city, and said to offer protection from fire.

Next stop, 200m (220yds) along the shore, is **Miniature Western Heaven** (Xiaoxitian), built in 1770. Aptly named, it was a shrine to Guanyin, the goddess of mercy. It's a large square pagoda surrounded by a moat and four guard towers. Backtrack to the **Five Dragon Pavilion** (Wulongting), named after the zigzagging walkways that link them.

Ferry to Jade Island

Just north of the Five Dragon Pavilion board a ferry to **Jade Island** (Qionghuadao; every half hour, 9am–6pm). The boat stops in front of Fangshan Restaurant, your dinner (or lunch) destination, but first explore the imperial gardens.

The restaurant is in the **Hall of Ripples** complex. Turn right on the covered walkway that leads to the **Pavilion of Shared Coolness**, and take the stone path leading up the hill. Climb to the **Plate for Gathering Dew**, there's a bronze figure of a man holding a container over his head. Emperor Qianlong built this whimsical tribute to a Han dynasty emperor who believed the dew was an elixir for immortality. Along the northwest side of the hill is the **Building for Reading Old Inscriptions** (Yuegulou), which has stone tablets covered with 6th- and 7th-century calligraphy. At the island's summit is the dazzling **White Dagoba** (Baita), a 35-m (115-ft) Buddhist shrine dating from 1651, built by the first Qing emperor to commemorate the first visit to Beijing by a Dalai Lama.

Descend the south side of the hill and pass through the **Hall of Universal Peace** (Pu'andian), an official meeting room in the Qing dynasty. Last is the Lamaist **Temple of Eternal Peace** (Yong'ansi). When you emerge at the south side of the island, you'll be facing an elegant marble bridge connecting the island to the shore. From here you can see, or cross the bridge to visit, the **Round Town** (Tuancheng; open daily 8.30am– 4.30pm; entrance fee). It used to be the administrative centre of the Mongol Yuan dynasty in 15th-century Dadu.

For dinner (or lunch), the **Fangshan Restaurant** (open daily 11am–1.30pm, 5–7.30pm; tel: 10-6401 1879) is definitely worth the walk around the perimeter of the island for its imperial cuisine. Try the sculpted beancurd with vegetables, or the bird's nest soup. Leave Beihai Park by the south gate, where taxis wait.

Top left: Lotus Flower Market vendor
Left: Nine Dragon Screen
Right: White Dagoba at Jade Island

9. PEKING DUCK AND PEKING OPERA *(see map, p18–19)*

A classic night on the town. Indulge in the ritual of eating Peking roast duck and then proceed to watch Peking opera.

Get to Tiananmen Square. Zhengyangmen Quanjude Roast Duck Restaurant is on the east side, just opposite the Monument to the Heroes of the People. Call ahead for reservations if you have a large group (14 Qianmen Xida-jie; tel: 10-6301 8833; open daily 11am–2pm, 5–7.30pm).

The earliest mention of Peking duck can be traced back to a 12th-century cookbook. The chefs from **Zhengyangmen Quanjude Roast Duck Restaurant** are schooled by Beijing's Quanjude masters, whose predecessors opened the famous Qianmen Quanjude Restaurant a few blocks to the south in 1864.

To prepare the ambrosial Peking duck, the bird's unbroken skin is inflated like a balloon, filled with water and glazed with sugar. The duck is then roasted in an oven heated by burning the wood of fruit trees such as date, peach and pear. This is done in order to impart a sweet, earthy aroma to the skin and flesh. When cooked, the crisp skin is sliced into bite-size pieces and served with a thin pancake, spring onion and a salty *hoisin* bean sauce. The rest of the duck meat is used in other dishes accompanying the meal. Part of the art of this cuisine is to make use of the entire duck, and this restaurant claims to make more than 300 different duck dishes, to be sampled while the duck is being roasted. If you're adventurous, try the cold mustard duck web, deep-fried duck liver with sesame and the fried duck hearts with chili sauce, but give the duck soup (à la dishwater) a miss.

When the roast duck arrives, you fill your own pancakes at the table. Use your chopsticks to pick up some spring onion and use it as a kind of paintbrush to dab some sauce on the pancake. Add one or two pieces of duck, roll the pancake, and *voila*! This is one of the rare times in China when using your fingers to eat is not considered impolite, so enjoy it. The cost of

Above: the art of make-up is all-important in Peking opera

a meal at the restaurant is approximately 80 yuan per person including a few different duck dishes and a drink.

Peking opera, or to be politically correct, Beijing opera, starts at 7.30pm at the Qianmen Hotel's **Liyuan Theatre** (75 Yongan Lu; performances daily 7.30–8.45pm; tel: 10-6301 6688 ext 8860), a 10-minute taxi ride from Qianmen. You can buy tickets from the booth next to the parking lot.

Peking opera is so highly stylised that you might assume it's an ancient art form, but in fact it was created in the late 18th century, drawing from several regional theatre forms. The result is a feast for the senses, though some foreigners find it an acquired taste. The singers use high-pitched voices and notes are strung out, the face-paint and costumes outrageous, and the action on stage accompanied by a piercing string and percussion ensemble.

Opera Conventions

In general, Peking opera can be classified into two types of stories – civilian and military. The Qianmen Hotel stages Peking opera mainly for foreign visitors, so they tend to choose action-packed martial stories, as well as excerpts from the classic novel *Journey to the West*, a popular Buddhist epic about the travels of the monk Tripitaka to seek Buddhist scriptures in India. These are great fun because the characters wear colourful costumes and there are plenty of acrobatics to dramatise battles. If you still have difficulty following the story, the English subtitles will help.

The characters with painted faces called *Jing* are warriors, heroes, statesmen, adventurers and supernatural beings. Good guys are generally painted with simpler designs, while more complicated patterns indicate enemy generals, bandits and robbers. Colours will tell if a character is courageous (red), cruel and conniving (oily white), wise (purple), or other-worldly (gold). Some painted designs tell a story, like the suns painted on the face of Hou Yi, the legendary character who shot down nine suns. Aside from the *Jing*, there are three main character types: *Dan*, a female lead role traditionally played by a man; *Sheng*, the male lead role; and *Chou*, the clown.

Much can be surmised from the body language of the performers, costumes, movements and props – all of which have set meanings. A single candle might represent evening, while a soldier carrying a banner represents an entire regiment. The flick of a sleeve expresses disgust. Like other traditional arts in China, Peking opera is losing ground to popular TV, film and music, but there is still a small, dedicated audience, mostly of older people, who relish it.

Other places to enjoy Peking opera, which are perhaps not as touristy as Liyuan Theatre, include **Changan Grand Theatre** (7 Jiannei Avenue; tel: 10-6510 1309 ext 10) and **Guanghe Theatre** (46 Qianmen Roushi Jie; tel: 10-6351 8284). Call in advance to check on the performance times.

Right: Peking duck

beijing & environs

10. TIANANMEN EVENING *(see map, p18–19)*

A sunset walk beginning with the flag-lowering ceremony on Tiananmen Square; then a walk by the moat of the Imperial Palace, ending with a visit to a night market, shopping in Wangfujing and to Sanlitun for its nightlife.

Take a taxi or pedicab to Tiananmen Square. Bus Nos 2, 10, 1, 4, 57, 20 and 52 also go there.

Tiananmen's flag-lowering ceremony happens at sunset, around 7.30pm in summer and 5.30pm in mid-winter. This is one of the few remaining Soviet-style rituals China still practises. To encourage patriotism after the Tiananmen crackdown in 1989, the ceremony was beefed up with more soldiers and a new taller flagpole. Hundreds gather each night to watch the military drill and flag-lowering, although it's hard to know precisely what draws them. A favourite pastime in Beijing is to *kan rinao*, which basically means to 'watch the excitement'. This could be anything from a lovers' tiff to a minor traffic accident. At any rate, soon after the flag descends, quiet settles over the square. At night, after the lights come up on the Monument to the People's Heroes and Tiananmen Gate, the square seems a very different place.

Gateway to the Forbidden City

Begin your walk by crossing under Dongchang'an Jie via the pedestrian tunnel, and then walking through **Tiananmen Gate**. The long approach from the gate, leading to the Meridian Gate (Wumen), the entrance to the Imperial Palace, is about 600m (656yds), at which point you will be forced to turn. Turn right and walk along the perimeter of the Imperial Palace, between its high wall and the moat. Strolling with just a few bicycles whirring past and lovers whispering on park benches, it is easy to imagine you have been transported back to a different century.

Go right, leave via the side gate

Above: Tiananmen Gate by night
Right: red bean porridge for supper

and take an immediate left. This road runs between the palace and the moat, so you cannot get lost. After 50m (55yds), it turns right, goes straight for another 400m (437yds) and turns left where there is another 50m (55yds) stretch. At this point you will see the east gate of the Imperial Palace on the left. The road bends right and becomes **Donghuamen Night Market**. Here, you will find some of the cheapest snacks in town. Try a bowl of red bean porridge or grilled quail if you're feeling peckish.

If you still need a full meal, you're in luck as you've just reached a strip of restaurants largely owned by and catering for overseas Chinese. There is good seafood and Cantonese fare on both sides of the street. Splurge on braised shark's fin with creamy crab sauce at the swanky **Hong Kong Food City** (on the right side; you can't miss the neon; 18 Dong'anmen Dajie; open daily 11am–2pm, 2.30–4pm; 5–9pm; tel: 10-6525 7349). Or try Mongolian hotpot at any one of the small restaurants along this stretch – you get plates of thinly-sliced raw meat and vegetables to plunge into a pot of boiling stock. Much of the pleasure derives from eating food you've just cooked yourself.

Shopping and Nightlife

If you feel up to it after dinner, continue walking east to **Wangfujing**, formerly the most prestigious shopping street in Beijing. The name dates back to the Yuan dynasty (1279–1368) when it was called Wang Fu Street. It was in the mid-Ming dynasty (1368–1644) when a well (*jing*) was discovered and the street became known as Wangfujing. By the late Qing dynasty (1644–1911), Wangfujing was a prosperous commercial thoroughfare. Many of many Beijing's old name brands can be found here. The street has now

become a pedestrian mall, flanked by shops and multi-storey shopping complexes. Walk along its length to observe the nouveau Chinese domestic tourists and consumers out for a stroll. Take a look inside the huge shopping malls to catch a glimpse of the future of Beijing.

If you still haven't had enough, hop into a taxi and check out the nightlife along Beijing's 'bar street', **Sanlitun**, located close to the City Hotel in the northeastern section of the city. Most of the bars and pubs are located to the north of the intersection with Gongrentiyuguan Beilu. The bars are lined up back to back along one side of the street and in the summer, depending on the local authorities, you can sit outside and watch the parade of people going from one bar to another. Sanlitun is very popular amongst locals and Beijing's large expatriate community, a combination reflected in the eclectic mix of Chinese and Western pop and rock music that blares out from most of the bars.

Right: street stalls, Donghuamen Night Market

Excursions

1. MING TOMBS AND THE GREAT WALL AT MUTIANYU
(see maps, p56 and 58)

A morning exploring the Ming tombs, followed by a picnic at the ruins. Then, a spectacular drive through the mountains and an afternoon hike on the Great Wall at Mutianyu. End the day by blasting away a few rounds on a sub-machine gun at the Great Wall Shooting Range. This is a full eight-hour day with strenuous walking.

Ask your hotel staff to help you rent a taxi for the day. This is a 185-km (115-mile) round trip and should cost 1–3 yuan per kilometre, depending on the vehicle. Make sure the cost, duration and itinerary are agreed in advance. And make sure your driver understands that you want to go to the Great Wall at Mutianyu, not the teeming Badaling section. A clearly marked road leads directly from the Ming Tombs to Mutianyu.

Of the 16 Ming emperors who reigned from 1368 to 1644, 13 were buried about 50km (30 miles) northwest of Beijing, in a natural amphitheatre formed by mountains on three sides. Heading due north from the Deshengmen Gate, you will retrace the route followed by the imperial dead to their final resting place. About 40km (25 miles) outside the city, you will pass through **Changping**, once a garrison town partly responsible for guarding the tombs. The town has a monument to the peasant leader Li Ziheng, who led the uprising that toppled the Ming dynasty in 1644.

Spirits of the Dead

When you reach the Ming Tombs (Shisanling; open daily 8am–6pm; entrance fee), enter through the **Spirit Way** (Shendao), the path over which the dead were carried during the funeral ceremony. It begins with a white stone portico a few kilometres north of Changping and stretches nearly 6km (4 miles) to the gate of the central tomb. The entrance to the imperial graveyard, which covers 15½ sq km (6 sq miles), is 500m (550yds) beyond the portico at the **Great Palace Gate** (Dagongmen).

Just beyond it is the entrance to the **Avenue of Stone Figures**. Ask the driver to let you walk and pick you up at the other end. Experts still debate the symbolism of these 24 carved stone creatures. Two of these, the *xiezhi* and *qilin*, are mythical animals that may have been placed there for luck. The more familiar elephants, camels and horses were probably meant to serve the emperors in the afterlife. Beyond the animals are 12 stone people: four fierce soldiers, four officials and four scholars.

Left: the Great Wall at Mutianyu
Right: Avenue of Stone Figures, Ming Tombs

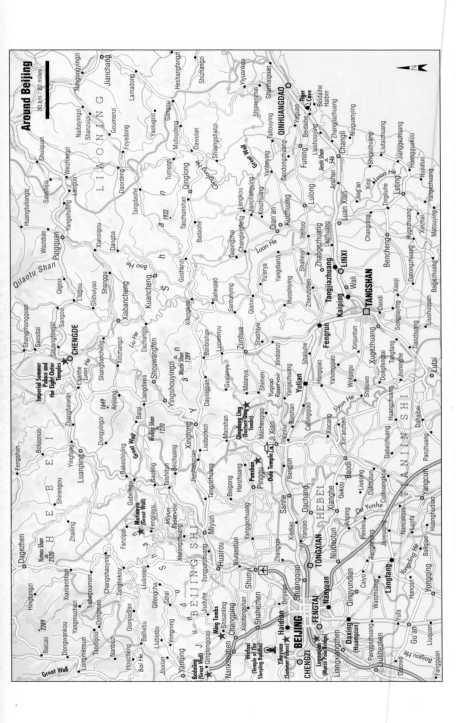

Three of the 13 tombs in this area are officially open as tourist sites: Dingling, Changling and Zhaoling. This excursion takes you to the first two, plus the ruins of another, Deling. Make your first stop about 10 minutes from the Avenue of the Animals at **Dingling** (open daily 8am–6pm), burial site of Emperor Wanli (1573–1619). His is the only tomb in this area that has been excavated. Wanli spent 8 million silver taels on his bid for immortality, enough to feed a million people for 6½ years at the time. It took 30,000 labourers six years to build the subterranean palace of five rooms with graceful arched ceilings – which were full of gold, silver, porcelain and jade treasures at one time.

Tombs with a View

To reach the vaults, cross the courtyard, climb the **Square Tower** (Fang Cheng) and follow the paths behind. The first room you enter has a pedestal that was intended for Wanli's concubines, but it was mysteriously empty when opened. According to one theory, this room was left empty for fear that repeated opening of the tomb would allow evil winds to disturb the emperor.

The next large room contains three stone altars, which were pushed up against the huge stone slab doors leading to the room where the coffins of Wanli and his two wives lay along with 26 treasure chests. Some of the

treasures are displayed at Changling, your next stop. More lasting is the architectural genius invested in the graves by the Ming emperors. The massive stone doors, now behind glass, were designed so that another stone slab slid into place when closed, locking them from the inside.

Move on to **Changling** (open daily 8am–6pm), a five-minute drive to the northwest. The burial place

Above: pavilion of the Great Stele
Left: Changling

of Emperor Yongle (1403–24), this is the best preserved of all the 13 tombs and a good example of how they were organised. In the front section, a large courtyard dominated by twisted pines leads to a sacrificial hall. The **Hall of Eminent Favours** (Ling'endian) is supported by 32 giant pillars, each carved from a single tree. The yellow glazed tiles and dragon head drains symbolise imperial majesty. A funeral tablet used to lay on a wooden altar at the centre of this room and sacrifices were made in front of it. The hall now contains an exhibition of items found in Dingling, from jewelled hairpins to suits of armour and the rich dragon brocade used in imperial dress.

Buried Pleasures

The second section is a courtyard in which a large stele marks the grave of the emperor. Just behind is the burial mound, enclosed by a wall about 500m (550yds) long. Presumably, this contains Emperor Yongle's coffin and burial treasures. To the east and west are burial grounds for his 16 concubines who, by some accounts, were buried alive to bring pleasure to the emperor in the next world.

Last stop at the tombs is Deling, where you part company with the vendors; you may want to buy drinks before leaving Changling. **Deling**, a 10-minute drive southwest, is where Wanli's grandson, Emperor Xi Zong (1621–27) is buried. Known as a keen carpenter but an inattentive ruler, Xi Zong lost power

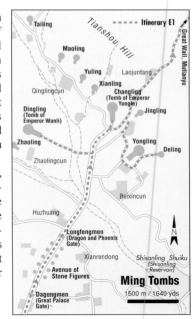

Above: unrenovated Ming Tombs

to his eunuchs. His dilapidated, overgrown tomb seems to reflect his downfall, with ceremonial urns strewn around as if after a brawl.

Backtrack to Changling. In the far corner of the car park, 100m (110yds) from the entrance, is a sign in Chinese saying 'Great Wall at Mutianyu 37km'. This is a beautiful drive eastward through villages and mountains. It is slightly further than the crowded Badaling section, but worth the effort.

You will spot the **Great Wall** long before you reach it. Adding together all the sections, it extends more than 3,860km (2,400 miles), twisting and doubling back from the coast all the way to the northwestern province of Gansu. Chinese tourist leaflets assert that this is the only man-made structure visible from the moon, but it is rumoured that New York's Staten Island garbage dump now shares the honour. Whatever the case, the Great Wall is a terrific lookout point for a soldier, or a tourist. The walk up to the wall takes a good 20 minutes, but you can avoid the climb by taking the cable car.

The 'Ten Thousand Li Great Wall', or *Wanli Chang Cheng* in Chinese, marked the peak of wall building in China. The wall originated as a labyrinth of smaller walls built by warring kingdoms in northern China from the 5th century BC. The first Qin emperor, Shi Huangdi, after unifying China in 221BC, made it his mission to link all the existing walls to create a single Great Wall against the barbarian tribes to the north.

Wall of Bones

Like the pyramids, the wall has its dark side. Hundreds of thousands of Chinese peasants were conscripted to build it, and many died in the process. Poets lamented the wall's 'bone core'. As many raids and later the full-scale Mongol invasion proved, a wall is only as strong as those who defend it. Nevertheless, once the Ming overthrew the Mongol Yuan dynasty, wall-building resumed with a vengeance. This was when the Great Wall took shape. **Mutianyu** and most other remaining sections date from the Ming period (1368–1644), when the wall was extensively repaired and fortified, with several new sections added. The restored Mutianyu section opened to tourists in 1986.

The road back to Beijing heads 75km (46 miles) due south, entering the city at Dongzhimen. If you have time, and need to relieve stress, stop on the way back at the **Beijing Great Wall Shooting Range** (open weekends only; reservations necessary; tel: 10-6964 3573), 14 km (9 miles) south of Mutianyu on a small road leading east. Try your hand at shooting clay pigeons or laser shooting, or a truly cathartic round on a sub-machine gun. The Great Wall Shooting Range is one of thousands of business ventures, including shops, factories and discos, opened by the Chinese military since the start of China's economic reforms.

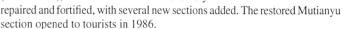

Right: the Great Wall at Mutianyu

2. BEIDAIHE BEACH *(see map, p56)*

A relaxing getaway to the seashore at Beidaihe on the Bohai Sea. This is an overnight trip because of the five-hour train ride.

Beijing Railway Station is located on Huochezhan Lu, south of Dongchang'an Jie, 2km (1¼ miles) east of Tiananmen Square. Several trains run to Beidaihe every day. Best is the express train, No 11, leaving at 8.30am and arriving Beidaihe at 12.45pm. The return express, No 12, leaves Beidaihe at 2pm and arrives in Beijing at 6.30pm. Tickets should be booked a few days in advance, either from the Foreigner's Booking Office at the station, or from a hotel travel service.

If you've conquered Beijing's temples, or they've conquered you, and you've had enough of the capital's crowds and traffic, then it's time for a day on the beach. The route to Beidaihe is a well-worn path for Beijing's officials. You'll see plenty of Mao suits and military uniforms with trousers rolled

up to the knees. Top leaders are usually cloistered away at a private beach south of town. The main beaches are packed during July and August but the beach area is kept remarkably clean. On the hills overlooking the Bohai Sea are mostly old brick villas with verandahs. A small boardwalk area is home to some good, inexpensive seafood restaurants.

Heavenly Hotels

Of the hotels open to foreigners, the best deal is the **Beidaihe Guesthouse for Diplomatic Missions**, (1 Baosan Lu; tel: 0335-404 1807 or 10-6532 4336 in Beijing), a five-minute walk from the main beach. It has friendly, English-speaking staff and a good seafood restaurant. All rooms have sea-facing balconies. At the high end is the **Jinshan Guesthouse** (4 Dongsan Lu; tel: 0335-404 1338). It's on a quiet beach 4km (2½ miles) north of town, with a business centre, bowling alley, and the works. For dinner, try the market on Shitang Lu for fresh, cheap seafood.

If you stay more than a night at Beidaihe, consider a day-trip to **Shanhaiguan**, 25km (16 miles) north along the coast and a one-hour ride by bus or taxi. Known as the 'First Pass Under Heaven', Shanhaiguan is a former garrison town on the Great Wall, just 4km (2½ miles) from the point where the wall meets the sea. The town walls are still intact, and a short distance inland there is a spectacular mountain section of the wall that is much quieter than the better known stretches near Beijing. The area is well worth visiting if you have the time.

Above: Beidaihe is one of China's most popular beach resorts

3. CHENGDE *(see maps, below and p56)*

An overnight stay in Chengde, the eclectic mountain retreat of the Qing emperors. With a four-hour train journey from Beijing, you might want to consider a second or even a third night at Chengde to cover its numerous and varied sights.

To get to Chengde, 250km (155 miles) north of Beijing, take the No 709 train from Beijing, which leaves at 7.20am and arrives at 11.20am. Buy your tickets from the Foreigners Booking Office at the Beijing Railway Station or have your hotel travel service purchase them for you. When leaving

Chengde, the No 710 departs at 2.40pm arriving in Beijing at 6.40pm. The railway station in Chengde is on the south side of town. Taxis, motorcycle taxis or bus Nos 2, 3 and 5 will take you to the Guesthouse for Diplomatic Missions, the Yunshan Hotel or the Palace Hotel.

Emperor Kangxi (1662–1722) of the Qing dynasty was drawn to the town of Jehol, as Chengde was called in the early 18th century, because of its location in a cool, lush valley with placid lakes and forests, 350m (1,148ft) above sea level. He ordered the building of the **Mountain Manor for Escaping the Summer Heat** (Bishushanzhuang) in 1703. It was also used in the later years of the Qing dynasty, when Emperor Qianlong (1736–96) expanded the residence, incorporating the styles of China's minorities in his sprawling kingdom as part of an effort to appease them.

Magical Retreat

In the Yanshan Mountains that surround the resort were 11 active temples, varying in architectural style. **Bishushanzhuang** (open daily 8am–6pm; entrance fee) is an excellent escape and a magical place to explore. If you have just one night in Chengde, spend the first afternoon strolling through Bishushangzhuang and save the more strenuous exploration of the temples for the next morning.

If you have more time, bizarre rock formations, caves and hot springs await you in the outlying areas. Chengde is quite compact and Bishushangzhuang can be reached easily by foot from the

Above: the Tower of Mist and Rain, Bishushanzhuang

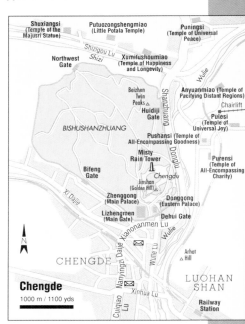

Shuxiangsi (Temple of the Majusri Statue)
Putuozongshengmiao (Little Potala Temple)
Puningsi (Temple of Universal Peace)
Shizigou Lu
Shizi
Northwest Gate
Xumifushoumiao (Temple of Happiness and Longevity)
Wulie
Beizhen Twin Peaks
Shanzhuang
Anyuanmiao (Temple of Pacifying Distant Regions)
Chairlift
Huidiji Gate
BISHUSHANZHUANG
Pulesi (Temple of Universal Joy)
Pushansi (Temple of All-Encompassing Goodness)
Misty Rain Tower
Donglu
Purensi (Temple of All-Encompassing Charity)
Bifeng Gate
Chengdu
Jinshan (Golden Hill)
Xi Dajie
Zhenggong (Main Palace)
Donggong (Eastern Palace)
Lizhengmen (Main Gate)
Dehui Gate
Xianonanmen Lu
Wulie
N
Nanyingzi Dajie
Wulie Lu
Arhat Hill
CHENGDE
LUOHAN SHAN
Chengde
1000 m / 1100 yds
Xinhua Lu
Cuiqiao Lu
Railway Station

hotels. Public buses and minibuses Nos 2, 3 and 5 also run up the main road, Wulie Jie, and stop next to the main gate of Bishushanzhuang.

Little in Chengde is translated for non-Chinese speakers. You may want to hire a guide through the local branch of the China International Travel Service (CITS; 11 Zhonghua Lu; tel: 0314-202 2274). The Yunshan Hotel can also arrange a guide.

Just inside the main gate is the **Bishushanzhuang Museum** (open daily 8am–5pm; entrance fee), which once housed the main palace. Laid out in the traditional linear style of halls and courtyards, it is made of unpainted wood and shaded by tall pines. The exhibits are varied: some rooms display items like Mongolian weapons and dress, others are set up as they were when they were used by the imperial court. Leaving by the back door of the museum takes you to the park proper. It is surrounded by a 10-km (6½-mile) wall and is the largest surviving imperial garden in China.

Pavilions and Pagodas

Off to the right, after 100m (110yds), begins a maze of paths, bridges, pavilions and halls surrounding several interlocking lakes. This area is for strolling, renting boats or gazing from park benches. Beyond it is the **Literary Nourishment Pavilion** (Wenjinge), one of four imperial libraries. Its central attraction is a rock garden where there is a special place for permanently 'viewing the moon', a trick of the light falling on the surrounding rock formations. At the far end of the east side of the park, you'll find a meadow marked by the pagoda of the **Temple of Eternal Blessing**, which was built by Emperor Qianlong for his mother's 50th birthday.

Heading left from the lake takes you into more rugged hiking area. Emperors Kangxi and Qianlong designated 72 scenic spots in Bishushanzhuang but you can find many more yourself. The hills are riddled with small temples and rock formations and topped by pavilion look-out points. A good place to relax and enjoy the greenery is the tea garden at the southeast corner of **Front Lake**, the main lake.

Get an early start on your second day and head for the temples (open daily 8am–5pm) beyond the walls of Bishushanzhuang. The best way to do this is to rent a taxi for the morning or day. Drivers know the circuit, but bring a tourist map. The temple tour also makes a strenuous but pleasant bike ride of about 25km (16 miles). There's a bike hire shop near the Yunshan Hotel.

The full circuit comprises the Eight Outer Temples, but start with these four and see how time and energy hold out. **Little Potala Temple** (Putuozongshengmiao; open daily 8am–5.30pm), which dates from 1767, is the largest and most spectacular complex, modelled on the Potala in Lhasa. The beautifully restored halls, staircases and walkways extend over a 22ha

Above: Tibetan architectural styles at Puningsi

excursions

(54 acre) hillside site. Tibetan-style prayer flags, banners and tapestries hang from the gleaming gold roofs of the temple. The design of the **Temple of Happiness and Longevity** (Xumisfushoumiao; open daily 8am–5.30pm), 1km (½ mile) east, is based on another Tibetan temple, at Shigatse. Built in 1779, it is still being restored. At its rear is one of the highlights, an octagonal pagoda commemorating the 70th birthday of Emperor Qianlong.

The **Temple of Universal Peace** (Puningsi; open daily 8am–5.30pm), 3km (2 miles) further northeast and built in 1755, stands out as it is a living monastery with about 50 lamas in residence. The second hall is laid out with long, low benches for religious study and ceremony. There is an amazing 22-m (72-ft) carved wooden statue of Guanyin, the Goddess of Mercy, with 42 arms and an eye on each palm (known as the Thousand Arm, Thousand Eye Guanyin). Finally, trek to the **Temple of Universal Joy** (Pulesi; open daily 8am–5.30pm), which lies due east of Bishushanzhuang. You'll find bronze images of the deities in various acts of passionate embrace and conquest of their enemies, great examples of the wonderful and terrifying imagery that comes with Tibetan Buddhism.

Club Peak Rock Formations

One of the strangest rock formations in the area is at **Club Peak**. You get there by taking a cable car from a few hundred metres north of Pulesi. It takes 20 minutes each way.

There are some good places to stay in Chengde, such as the **Yunshan Hotel** (6 Nanyuan Jie, Nanyuan Donglu; tel: 0314-202 4657) and the **Chengde Guesthouse for Diplomatic Missions** (Wulie Jie, Central Section; tel: 0314-202 5179). For traditional atmosphere try the **Qianwanglou Hotel**, (Bifengmen Lu; tel: 0314-202 4358), a reproduction of a Qing-dynasty mansion. A different option, if you're visiting between March and October, is the **Mongolian Yurt Holiday Village** (tel: 0314-216 2710). Inside the imperial resort grounds, you stay in circular Mongolian tents (yurts). It's not real camping as the yurts are air-conditioned and have baths and television sets, but it's fun.

Local cuisine centres mainly on wild game, as the area was reserved as the emperor's hunting ground. Try **Huanggong Yushanfang** at the **Palace Hotel** (21 Wulie Jie; tel: 0314-202 5092). Women dressed as Qing dynasty maids serve venison, wild boar and pheasant. Ask for prices in advance; they're not listed on the menu. Staying in your hotel for meals is a safe, but less interesting, option; there are snack vendors and restaurants near the temples and Bishushanzhuang, but these would not win any awards for cleanliness.

Above: Club Peak
Left: Mongolian-style yurt

Leisure Activities

SHOPPING

Forget any notion you had about an austere workers' paradise. Consumerism is the only meaningful 'ism' in Beijing these days. The number of *dakuan* – fat cats with cellphones – is exploding. Russian traders are flooding into Beijing for goods, and more and more ordinary people have hard cash instead of the grain coupons they once held. New markets, stores and restaurants open almost every day. 'Socialism with Chinese characteristics', as the government calls its Byzantine economy with its own rules.

It's advisable to first check prices at state stores before buying a similar item in a hotel shop or free market. Some rules: bargain hard; be stubborn but friendly if you're interested in something; and try not to appear too keen. Make your first offer no more than 50 percent of the shopkeeper's initial asking price, and expect to finally pay 50–70 percent of the asking price. If buying several things from one store, you should get a better deal. Be persistent, keep smiling and walk away if you find the price unacceptable.

Speciality Markets and Stores

If shopping is your favourite hobby, you'll be in good company in Beijing's bustling markets. The **Silk Market** (Xiushui Shichang; open daily 9am–6pm) on Xiushui Jie, which intersects with Jianguomenwai Avenue about 800m (875yds) east of the Friendship Store, is the most popular place to buy clothes for Beijing's foreign residents and tourists.

Many stalls stock silk dresses, shirts, jackets, ties, boxer shorts and nightgowns; but they also have down jackets, designer labels (some fake, most genuine or pirated), traditional Chinese-style clothes, wool sweaters, cotton shorts and T-shirts, fashion boots and souvenirs. Although you won't find any on display, you will probably be offered pirated CDs, VCDs and CD-ROMs.

These are very inexpensive but the quality is often poor. And there is always the possibility that pirated CD-ROMs are infected with nasty computer viruses.

There are several other good places to buy silk fabrics: **Friendship Store** (17 Jianguomenwai Dajie; open daily 9am–9pm); **Yuan Long Silk Store** (North Gate of the Temple of Heaven; open daily 9am–6.30pm); and **Ruifuxiang Silk and Cotton Fabric Store** (Old Outer City; open daily 9am–7.30pm).

Just a few blocks away from the Silk Market on Ritan Lu, opposite the west side of Ritan Park, is **Yabalou Market**, also popularly known as the Russian Market (open daily 9.30am–6pm). This is another huge and growing clothes market specialising in modern, factory-made cotton, wool and down garments.

Hongqiao Market (open daily 8.30am–7pm), on Tiantan Lu opposite the east gate of the Temple of Heaven, has the best collection of antique clocks and Mao statues, as well as freshwater pearls and inexpensive reproduction antiques *(see also page 35)*.

For traditional Chinese paintings, calligraphy supplies and rare books, poke around the Qing dynasty-style stores on **Liulichang** (open daily 9.30am–5.30pm), just west of the Qianmen area *(see also page 46)*. Further afield, but considered the most reliable source of antique porcelain in Beijing is **Panjiayuan Market** (open daily 9.30am–6.30pm) located on the Third Ring Road East at the Jingsong east junction. Much like a flea market, the outdoor stalls at Panjiayuan cover a large area and a large variety of objects. Most of the ceramic items on sale are reproductions, some openly so, others masquerading as

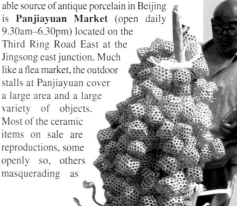

Left: souvenir masks
Right: market vendor selling crickets

the real thing. But among these are many genuine antiques and curios, as well as a large 'junk' section next door where you can buy anything from plastic bathtubs to used bicycle bearings. Another place to look for curios is the **Beijing Antique Curios City** (Beijing Gu Wan Cheng), located at West Huawei Bridge, Dongnansanhuan (open daily 9.30am–6pm).

If you are looking for that extra special Chinese art-inspired museum shop-type gift, you can call **Cultural Imprints** (tel: 10-6528 3529, 6523 7577), an export company that sells high quality *objets d'art*. They have no retail space but will organise a visit to their showroom upon request. Gifts include silk, paper and porcelain.

Note: Antiques that date from prior to 1975 may not be exported legally. Those that can be taken out of China must carry a small red seal or sticker, or have one affixed by the Cultural Relics Bureau. Beware of fakes: producing new 'antiques' (and the seal) is a thriving industry in China.

Non-Tourist Shopping Spots

Three lively shopping streets cater for a large proportion of Beijing's local and visiting shoppers. **Wangfujing, Xidan** and **Dongdan** all run north from Dongchang'an Jie. They all sell mostly inexpensive local goods, with bargains in leather and other clothing. At 192 Wangfujing Dajie, check out the **Jianhua Leather Goods Company** (open daily 9am–8.30pm). It covers everything from basic leather jackets for as little as 500 yuan to full-length mink coats at up to 30,000 yuan. You'll also find suede backpacks, belts and fox pelts. Further north, on the east side of Wangfujing is the **Foreign Languages**

Bookstore (235 Wangfujing Dajie; open daily 9am–6pm). The first floor has a wide range of books on China in English, on subjects like Chinese acupuncture, painting, medicine, philosophy and language. The upper floors are crammed with text books, imported books, stationery, computers and a music store. All three streets are undergoing radical transformation, with more and more upscale department stores, boutiques and watch stores being built.

Among the most popular department stores for Chinese products is **Longfu Dashsa** (95 Longfusi Jie, Chaoyang; open daily 9am–8.30pm). Here you can buy China's best-known brands of household products, such as Flying Pigeon bicycles and Butterfly sewing machines.

One-stop Shopping

Beijingers love shopping, and have readily embraced the new glossy joint-venture shopping centres that sell everything, including overpriced imported products.

Almost opposite the Friendship Store on Jianguomenwai Dajie is the **Scitech Plaza** (22 Jianguomenwai Dajie; open daily 9.30am–10pm) shopping centre, full of luxury items, including many designer label clothing outlets. **Yan Sha Youyi Shopping City** (52 Liangmaqiao Lu; open daily 9am–9pm), which opened in 1992 at the Beijing Lufthansa Centre, carries products with a broader price range. The store stocks one of Beijing's best selections of silk by the metre at reasonable prices.

Stock up on all the beautiful things that China produces, like traditional paper cuttings (inexpensive and easy to pack), jade carvings, kites and chopsticks, at the state-run Friendship Store at 17 Jianguomenwai Dajie (open daily 9am–9pm). This is also a good place to get a benchmark on prices before you haggle at the markets.

Several ultra modern and fashionable malls have opened over the past few years in Beijing. The **Palace Hotel Shopping Arcade** (8 Jingyu Hutong; open daily 9am–9pm) and the **China World Trade Centre Shopping Centre** (1 Jianguomenwai Dajie; open daily 9am–9pm) with its sprawling underground mall are both upmarket places with a wide range of imported goods.

Above: ceramics in Liulichang

EATING OUT

In China, when people greet each other on the street, instead of inquiring 'How are you?' they ask 'Have you eaten?' Food is an obsession in China, probably because not so long ago most people didn't get enough to eat. Whatever the reason, the culinary arts are highly valued and varied. The range of eating options is enormous, from street vendors roasting sweet potatoes for a few yuan to Western restaurants dishing up meals that would gobble up the average local worker's monthly salary in one go. For the tourist, Beijing offers the opportunity to taste dishes from all over China at reasonable prices. Hotels and the many independent restaurants serve a wide range of cuisines for the homesick palate.

The approximate cost of a meal per person is categorised as follows:

$ = 50–100 yuan;
$$ = 100–200 yuan;
$$$ = more than 200 yuan.

Beijing and Imperial Cuisine

Many dishes classified as Beijing-style actually originated from other parts of the kingdom, and were perfected and embellished at the imperial court. Beijing cuisine makes liberal use of strong flavours like garlic, ginger, spring onion and coriander. The dishes of the north tend to be heartier, with noodles and steamed or fried bread as the staple, rather than rice.

Jianbing, Beijing's most popular street snack, originated in Tianjin. It is a kind of pancake made with egg and spring onion, filled with crunchy, deep-fried dough sticks and garnished with chili sauce and coriander. The most famous Beijing dish is Peking duck, a whole meal with many dishes featuring every part of the duck *(see page 50)*. Another popular meal, especially in winter, is Mongolian hotpot – slivers of mutton plunged into a trough of boiling water, fondue-style. The hotpot restaurants usually have a picture of a hotpot on their windows.

Fangshan Restaurant

Qionghua Dao, Beihai Park, Xicheng
Tel: 10-6401 1879
Garden setting at Beihai Park. If you want to enjoy a somewhat authentic Qing atmosphere, service and presentation, the only restaurant remaining in Beijing that can do the job is this one. Please note, however, that Qing court cuisine does not always appeal to modern taste buds. Open daily 11.30am–1.30pm; 5–7pm. $$

Li Family Restaurant

11 Yongfang Hutong, Deshengmennei Dajie,
Xicheng
Tel: 10-6618 0107
Serves four tables of up to 12 each day – two at lunch and two at dinner in the home of the chef, who has a story for each dish. Must book ahead. Open daily 6–10pm. $$$

Old Beijing Noodle King

29 Chongwenmen Wai Dajie, Chongwen
Tel: 10-6705 6705
Close to the Temple of Heaven, this restaurant has revived the lively tradition of Beijing fast food. Waiters bellow at the diners to announce the arrival or departure of each customer. Try the tasty noodles, usually eaten with a thick sesame and soy-based sauce. Look for the rickshaws outside. $

Above: Beijing-style dishes

Peking Duck Restaurants
Tuanjiehu Peking Roast Duck Restaurant
3 Tuanjiehu Beikou, Dongsanhuan
Tel: 10-6507 2892
At one of the classiest of duck restaurants, every part of the duck is served in a range of exquisite side dishes including deep-fried heart with coriander and stir-fried intestines. The roast duck is a little crisper than that of many competitors. *$$$*

Zhengyangmen Quanjude Roast Duck Restaurant
East side of Tiananmen Square,
14 Qianmen Xidajie
Tel: 10-6301 8833
Clean and well-run, with more than 300 duck dishes. The original chefs were trained by Beijing's Quanjude masters, whose predecessors opened the famous Qianmen Quanjude Roast Duck Restaurant, a few blocks to the south, in 1864. Open daily 11am–2pm; 5–7.30pm. *(see pages 50–51.) $$*

Shandong Cuisine
Dishes from neighbouring Shandong province are the main element in what Beijingers call home cooking. The number of restaurants serving this fare outnumber any other kind. Since Shandong is a coastal province, seafood such as tiger prawns, eel, shark's fin and sea cucumber feature largely in the dishes.

Confucian Heritage Restaurant
3 West Liulichang Jie, Liulichang
Tel: 10-6303 0689
An inviting two-storey teahouse in the historical Liulichang area. A good array of dishes from Shandong. *$–$$*

Cui Hua Lou Restaurant
58 Wangfujing Jie, Dongcheng
Tel: 10-6526 4581
Shandong dishes served amid a lively setting, decorated in the traditional style. Seafood figures prominently on the menu. Open daily 7am–10pm. *$$*

Sichuan Cuisine
The densely populated southwestern province of Sichuan is famous for its spicy food, which, it is said, matches the temperament of its people. Sichuan restaurants are found everywhere in Beijing, and Sichuan dishes are standard on most menus in small, non-specialised restaurants. Chicken, pork and freshwater fish are favourite ingredients, and noodles, bread and rice are all served. Try some *dandan mian* (hot spicy noodles) or *la mian* (cold spicy noodles), peppery fish-head soup, or the sizzling rice-crust dish called *guo ba*.

Sichuan Restaurant
Jia 14, Liuyin Jie, Xicheng
Tel: 10-6615 6925

Above: clear soups are typically Chinese

Formerly located in a *hutong* behind the Great Hall of People, and frequented by the former Chinese Premier Deng Xiaoping, this well-known restaurant can now be found near Prince Gong's Palace, north of Beihai lake. The food is still as delicious. Try the Sichuan spicy and sour soup, and diced chicken with hot peppers. Reservations advised. Open daily 11am–2pm; 5–9pm. *$$*

Jin Shan Cheng

2nd Floor, Zhongfu Daxia, across from the China World Hotel
Tel: 10-6581 6188 ext 2131
Lively, noisy atmosphere. Delicious, authentic, spicy Sichuan food. Try the *laziji* if you like mounds of sautéed red chili peppers with morsels of chicken. The *shuizhu niurou* (beef slices in spicy soup) is also good. Open daily 11am–2pm; 5–10pm. *$*

Cantonese Cuisine

Cantonese food is known for its delicate flavours and fresh ingredients, preferably bought the same day and cooked briskly before serving, using little oil or spice. *Dim sum* – rice-flour or bread parcels filled with meat, seafood, or vegetables – are meant to be snacks but come in so many varieties that a *dim sum* lunch often turns into a feast. Many excellent Cantonese restaurants have sprung up in Beijing, but they tend to be more expensive than other Chinese restaurants.

Windows On The World

28/F CITIC Building, 19 Jianguomenwai Dajie, Chaoyang East
Tel: 10-6500 3355
Excellent *dim sum* served in a pleasant dining room with good views west over the city. The dinner menu is more extensive and features a wide variety of regional specialities. Open daily 11.30am–2.30pm; 5.30–10pm. *$$$*

Four Seasons

1/F Jianguo Hotel, 5 Jianguomenwai Dajie, Chaoyang East
Tel: 10-6500 223, ext 8041
Quiet, classical setting enhances the fine and delicate flavours of Cantonese food. Fresh fish, lightly steamed in soya sauce, and stir fried vegetables are winners. Open daily 11.30am–2.30pm; 5.30–10pm. *$$$*

Other Chinese Cuisines

Afanti

2 Houguaibang Hutong, Chaoyangmennei Dajie, Dongcheng
Tel: 10-6525 1071
Lively Xinjiang restaurant serving sumptuous roast lamb, kebabs and flatbreads. Accompained by live Uighur and Uzbek music and dance. Reservations advised. Open daily 11am–midnight. *$$*

Tibet Shambala

301 Xinjiang Xiao Lu, Baishiqiao, Haidian
Tel: 10-6842 2631
The Tibetan owner has attempted to bring a touch of high-plains cuisine to far-off Beijing. Diners sit in small whitewashed rooms draped with Tibetan Buddhist paintings. Try *tsampa* (barley flour blended with yak butter), *momos* (dumplings filled with minced yak meat) and *thukpa* (noodles with lamb). *$$*

Nengrenju

5 Taipingqiao, Baitasi, Xicheng
Tel: 10-6601 2560
Many claim Nengrenju is the best hotpot restaurant in Beijing, with good service and fine food. Take the plunge with several curls of finely sliced lean lamb. After that, select from the restaurant's fine array of seafood, mushrooms, vegetables, noodles, beancurd and many other ingredients. *$$*

Gongdelin

158 Qianmen Nan Dajie, Qianmen
Tel: 10-6511 2542
Beijing's most famous vegetarian restaurant. The Beijing branch of a Shanghai restaurant which opened in the early 1920s, Gongdelin specialises in amazing mock meat dishes, carefully crafted from beancurd, mushrooms and vegetables. A few dishes are so realistic that some vegetarians are put off by the appearance. Open daily 10.30am–1.30pm; 4.30–8pm. *$*

Daijiacun Restaurant

Guandongdian Nanjie, Chaoyang
Tel: 10-6714 0145
Yunnanese food, much of it from the southwestern province's numerous minorities, is served here. The emphasis is on fresh herbs

and the use of coconut. There are also nightly performances of Yunnan dancing and singing while you eat. Reservations are strongly advised. *$$*

Other Asian Cuisines
Nadamen
2F, China World Hotel, 1 Jianguomenwai Dajie, Chaoyang East
Tel: 10-6505 2266 ext 39
This is as close as you are going to get to authentic Japanese food and presentation in Beijing. There is a beautiful atmosphere, reminiscent of Kyoto *ryokan*. Delicate sushi, delicious noodle dishes and wonderfully crisp tempura. Open daily 11.30am–2pm; 5.30–9.30pm. *$$$*

Omar Khayyam
Asia Pacific Building, 8 Yabao Lu, Chaoyang Northeast
Tel: 10-6513 998 ext 20188
Beijing's finest Indian cuisine, served in very pleasant surroundings. Sample delicious yoghurt-laced curries and authentic tandoori dishes. Open daily 11.30–2.30pm; 6–10.30pm. *$$*

Red Basil Thai Restaurant
8 Nanxiao Jie, Dongsanhuan Beilu (3rd Ring Road; south of San Yuan Bridge)
Tel: 10-6460 2342
Excellent food and efficient, friendly service in the capital's most celebrated Thai restaurant. Hearty *tom yam* soup and green chicken curry are firm favourites of the house. Open daily 11.30–2pm; 5.30–10pm. *$$*

Star of Asia
26 Dongsanhuan Beilu (3rd Ring Road)
Tel: 10-6582 5360
Serves an array of Asian cuisines, including Malaysian, Thai, Indian and Chinese. The dishes range from very spicy to delicately mild. Reservations advised. Open daily 11–2.30pm; 5–10.30pm. *$$*

Western
Bleu Marine
5 Dongdaqiao Lu, Chaoyang East
Tel: 10-6500 6704
The chefs buy fresh ingredients daily and the exquisite French menu changes regularly. The authentic atmosphere is irresistible to homesick Europeans. Reservations essential. Open Mon–Sat 11.30am–3pm; 6.30–10.30pm. *$$$*

Courtyard
95 Donghuamen, Dongcheng
Tel: 10-6526 8882
A renovated courtyard-type house, with sleek modern interior, skylights and a cigar lounge. The chic restaurant overlooks the moat of the Imperial Palace. Serves well prepared East-West fusion cuisine in an atmosphere of casual elegance. Downstairs is a contemporary Chinese art gallery. This is an oasis if you need to be pampered. Reservations recommended. Open daily for lunch and dinner. *$$$*

Ashanti
Opposite North Gate of Worker's Gymnasium, 168 Xing Zhong Jie, Chaoyang Northeast
Tel: 10-6416 6231
Warm atmosphere and good Spanish food. Unusual decor of contemporary Chinese oil paintings and Chinese furniture with Latin warmth. Reservations recommended. Open daily 6pm–midnight. *$$*

Mexican Wave
Eastside, Dongdaqiao Lu, Chaoyang East
Tel: 10-6506 3961
A long-time expat favourite, serving up not only Mexican standards such as enchiladas and tortillas, but also decent pizzas and hamburgers. Open daily 11.30am–midnight. *$$*

Left: breakfast at a street stall

NIGHTLIFE

'Beijing nightlife' was once a contradiction in terms, but as China opens up and its people have more time and money for leisure, even the puritanical capital is beginning to shake a little. Some traditional forms of entertainment, like the teahouse and the night market, are reviving. New forms, especially pubs, discos and pop concerts, have caught on among the younger and more affluent population.

If you want to do as Beijingers do, the first place to go is where the food is: night markets and private restaurants. Night markets are fair weather spots where you can sit outside, eat snacks and swill cool beer. When the weather's colder, seek out Mongolian hotpot, which follows the Chinese proverb of 'making one thing serve two purposes' by warming your hands as you cook your own dinner.

Ballroom dancing made a strong comeback in the 1980s and remains popular among middle-aged and elderly people. Karaoke, which took Beijing by storm in the 1990s, is, however, no longer fashionable among the city's hip and trendy. Cinemas are plentiful but movies are a hit and miss affair. Famous Chinese art house films shown in the West, like *Farewell My Concubine* or *Raising the Red Lantern*, are not typical of the Chinese and Western action movies shown in most cinemas in Beijing.

Discos have proliferated and major hotels are beefing up their live offerings with local and overseas acts. Many of the leading hotels have their own discos, and there are plenty of popular independent venues. A number of local entrepreneurs have opened rock venues, and Beijing is becoming a regular stop-off on the international circuit.

Beijing remains a casual place. Formal dress is not required anywhere, though neatness is appreciated in expensive hotels and restaurants. For such a large city, Beijing is very safe, but take the usual precautions with valuables as the number of pickpockets appears to be increasing. Men alone or in groups should beware of 'clip joints', bars in which hostesses will join you for a drink and later demand huge fees for their 'services'.

Gay bars or nightclubs, as with most other Asian countries, tend to be low key and underground. There are a few uniquely gay watering holes, but the locations do change on occasion. It's best to surf the Internet for information before arriving in China to see what is on and where. You can always try Drag-on, located on the main street in Maizidian, No 73. It's a street that runs along the south side of the Great Wall Sheraton.

Apart from the suggestions here, check out local English-language publications for tourists and expats, such as *City Weekend*, *BLT*, *Beijing This Month*, *Beijing Info* and

Above: a Beijing disco scene

China Daily's Beijing Weekend. All are available at most hotels. Or check these web listings: www.xianzai.com, www.cityweekend.com.cn, www.metronet.com.cn, www.chinabuzz.com. Tickets for many cultural events in Beijing, including theatre, music, ballet and Peking opera, can be bought online from www.webtix.com.cn.

Night Markets
Lotus Flower Market
Southwest shore of Qianhai Lake
Authentic Beijing-style local night market with great bustling atmosphere. Closes around midnight.

Donghuamen Market
One block west of Palace Hotel
Offers good range of Beijing snacks, as well as lamb kebabs and Cantonese sweets. Closes about 10pm.

Ballroom Dancing
Yueli Yuan Flower Garden
Ditan Park
Live band with music ranging from disco to waltz. Good clean fun. Open daily 7.30–9.30pm, if weather permits, March to mid-October.

Zhongshan Park
Enter from Dongchang'an Jie, just west of Tiananmen Gate
Tel: 10-6605 5431 ext 258
Indoor and outdoor dance floors. Open daily 2.30–5.30pm; 7.30pm–midnight.

Bars and Pubs
Arcadia (Tian Yu)
Jindu Apartments, Fangchengyuan Block 3, Fangzhuang
Tel: 10-6764 8271
Modern abstract decor; live Chinese rock bands every Friday and Saturday. Located in southeast Beijing near Longtan Park. Open daily 10am–midnight.

Jam House
Sanlitun Nan Jiuba Jie, Chaoyang
Tel: 10-6506 3845
Chinese and expat bands play all kinds of Western and Chinese pop in a bar frequented by young foreigners.

Pretty Bird
Anhuali Xiqu, behind the Jiangsu Hotel
Tel: 10-6427 7025
A former bomb shelter now houses a cavernous club full of experimental sculpture and experimental people.

Big Easy
Chaoyang Park, South Gate
Tel: 10-6508 6776
Beijing's best jazz bar, styled as a house in French New Orleans. Open daily 5pm–2am.

Hard Rock Café
8 Dongsanhuan Beilu (3rd Ring Road)
Tel: 10-6590 6688 ext 2571
The food and loud music are typical of every Hard Rock Café in the world. Live bands most nights. Open daily 10.30am–midnight.

Minder Café
Dongdaqiaoxie Jie, Sanlitun, Chaoyang
Tel: 10-6500 6066
A meeting place for Beijing's young expats; raucous at weekends. Resident Filipino band. Open daily till 2am.

Sanwei Bookstore
60 Fuxingmenwai Dajie, Fengtai
Tel: 10-6601 3204
Traditional teahouse above bookshop. Friday is jazz night, Saturday is Chinese classical music. Open daily 9.30am–10.30pm.

Frank's Place
Gongren Tiyuguan Donglu, Chaoyang
Tel: 10-6507 2617
All American watering hole with great burgers, taco chips and, of course, a wide selection of beers. Open daily 9am–midnight.

Paulaner Brauhaus
Beijing Lufthansa Centre, Dongsanhuan Beilu (3rd Ring Road)
Tel: 10-6465 3388 ext 5734
Serves real German beer brewed in-house, and tasty German food. Open daily 11–1am.

Discos
The Den
4A Gongti Donglu, next to the City Hotel
Tel: 10-6592 6290
Restaurant-cum-disco, open for lunch and

dinner; 70's and 80's house music. Popular among young Chinese and expats. Fills up around midnight. Open daily 1pm–3am.

Hot Spot
North side of Dong Sanhuan, Chaoyang
Tel: 10-6501 9933
A well-established favourite, this frenetic disco with caged dancers and karaoke singers attracts affluent young Chinese, even though it is owned, oddly enough, by the PLA. Free entry for foreigners. Open daily 8.30pm–2am.

The Loft
off Gongti Beilu, next to Pacific Place
Tel: 10-6501 7501

Contemporary cavernous loft space, video walls, underlit floor and galvanised Ming-style chairs. Serves Western food. Also a popular bar spot and, after 10pm, a disco. There is an outdoor garden as well. Open daily 11pm–2am.

Nightman
2 Xibahenanli, Chaoyang
Tel: 10-6466 2522
Young Chinese and Westerners dance non-stop to hip-hop, house, techno and everything else served up by the foreign DJs. Now somewhat rundown and out of fashion. Free entry for foreigners. Open daily 8pm–3am.

Rock N' Roll
Chaoyang Park South Gate,
1 Nongzhanguan Nanlu
Tel: 10-6592 9856
On the edge of Chaoyang Park, the massive complex is packed with Beijingers gyrating to the latest disco tunes. You can play pool as well in an attached pub. Open daily 8pm–5am.

Vogue
88 Gongti Donglu, diagonally across from City Hotel
Tel: 10-6416 5316
Hip loft-like space, with mezzanine balcony lounge overlooking dance floor. A place for the 'in' and beautiful expats and Chinese. Weekends crowded. Open 7pm–5am.

Traditional Theatre and Shows
Chaoyang Theatre
36 Dongsanhuan Beilu, Chaoyang
Tel: 10-6507 2421
Nightly at 7.15pm, spectacular individual and team acrobatic displays performed by very nimble artistes.

China Puppet Theatre
1 Anhuaxili
Tel: 10-6425 4849
Traditional stories acted out by shadow- and hand-puppets. Performances on Sat and Sun only, 9.30–10.30am; 10.30–11.50am.

Lao She Teahouse
3/F, 3 Qianmenxi Dajie, Qianmen
Tel: 10-6303 6830
Performances include excerpts from Peking opera, acrobatics, magic and comedy.

Liyuan Theatre
75 Yongan Lu, Qianmen Hotel
Tel: 10-6301 6688 ext 8860
Popular Peking opera venue and a good introduction to this ancient form of Chinese theatrical arts. Performances daily 7.30–8.45pm.

Zhengyici Theatre
220 Xiheyan Dajie, Hepingmen Wai, Zhengyici, Juchang
Tel: 10-6303 3104
Old wooden theatre used as an opera venue.

Above: Chaoyang acrobats

CALENDAR OF EVENTS

Whenever you arrive in China, it will be close to an official holiday or traditional festival. Holidays such as National Day (October 1) and International Labour Day (May 1) are fixed, but traditional festivals are set according to the lunar calendar and so vary from year to year. Dates for these celebrations, and information on annual events like the Beijing Marathon, can be obtained through the Beijing branch of the China International Travel Service (CITS) (Tourism Building, 28 Jianguomenwai Dajie; tel: 10-6515 8264).

January/February

The new calendar year begins with the tolling of the bell at the Big Bell Temple (Dazhongsi) and a one-day public holiday. The western new year is growing in popularity, with TV specials and parties at the Great Wall. But the biggest bash remains the lunar new year, known as **Spring Festival** or, in the West, as **Chinese New Year**. It normally starts in late January or early February. The date varies because it is traditionally set so that it falls on the second new moon after the winter solstice. Every December and January, public buildings are festooned with lights and banners. People across China travel to see their families, debts are settled, and the making and buying of food and drink builds toward its frenetic climax. In northern China, a holiday staple is boiled *jiaozi* (pasta parcels similar to ravioli). Both eating *jiaozi* and gathering family and friends to help with the time-consuming process of making them are important Spring Festival traditions. At midnight on the eve of the Spring Festival, firecrackers still sound across the city (in defiance of a ban) and there are large pub-

lic fireworks displays. On the first day of the lunar year, people don their best clothes and go out to visit friends and relatives. Traditionally, everyone, no matter how poor, must put on new clothes to usher in good luck in the new year. In recent years, a more relaxed atmosphere has seen the return of old traditions such as giving *hongbao* (little red envelopes containing money) to children. Beijing's 'little emperors' (pampered children), now usually expect at least 50 yuan. Throughout the Spring Festival week, temple fairs at Longtan Park and Ditan Park feature folk dancing, opera, martial arts, comedy, food and toy stalls. The fairs at Taoist Baiyunguan, Tibetan-Buddhist Yonghegong and other temples are mainly religious and are very popular among locals.

Beijingers, who have an amazing resilience to the bitter winters, relish ice-skating, sledding and winter swimming. Many lakes and canals, including Kunming Lake at the Summer Palace and the moat of the Imperial Palace, are used as skating rinks. Throughout the winter, Longqing Gorge outside Beijing holds its **Ice Lantern Festival**.

March/April

March brings a breather for Chinese women. **International Women's Day** on March 8 is an official holiday for those who 'hold up (more than) half the sky'.

On the 12th day of the third lunar month people honour their dead relatives by observing **Qingming**, sometimes referred to as the 'grave-sweeping' day.

With spring comes the **Beijing International Kite Festival** at the Mentougou Sports Centre, staged for five days in mid-April. Beijing's leading kite-makers show off their elaborate dragon kites alongside hi-tech stunt kites from abroad. The tradition of kite-flying dates back at least 2,500 years in China.

In late April and early May, the Beijing Botanical Gardens, close to Fragrant Hills Park, bursts into a riot of colours for the **Peach Blossom Festival**.

May/June

International Labour Day is a one-day public holiday, much more low-key since the economic reforms, with no more massive military parades. Following hot on its heels is

Above: a Spring Festival fair

Youth Day, a commemoration of the May Fourth Movement of 1919, reflected mainly by editorials and government support in the Chinese media. However, since 2000, the official holiday period starting from May 1 is seven days long. The domestic tourist industry literally takes off, so if you are planning to travel during these days, plan in advance.

International Children's Day is celebrated in earnest on June 1, by letting out classes early and treating children to outings to a park or zoo.

The crushing of the Tiananmen Square protests on June 4 1989 is not, of course, officially marked, but it is not forgotten either. Extra uniformed and plain-clothes police officers are stationed around the city.

To beat the dog days of summer, a new Water Melon Festival takes place in Daxing county, outside Beijing, at the end of June, right up to the first week of July.

July/August

July 1 is the Anniversary of the Founding of the Communist Party, which began in Shanghai in 1921. Celebrations include banquets held for important party members.

The fifth day of the fifth lunar month, usually late July, brings the Dragon Boat Festival, marked in Beijing by international dragon boat races. The festival has been celebrated since China's earliest times and a number of legends are associated with it. Triangular *zongzi*, sticky rice cakes wrapped in bamboo leaves, used to be thrown into the river where a famous poet is said to have hurled himself overboard. Today, *zongzi* are eaten to mark the occasion. The location of the boat races change each year. Check tourist publications or your hotel information desk.

From late July through early September, Beijing celebrates the Lantern Festival in Beihai and other parks. The festival dates back 3,000 years and is believed to be connected with the lifting of evening curfew for a few days at this time of year. Elaborate home-made lanterns light up the streets.

August 1 is the Anniversary of the People's Liberation Army. The date can be seen in Chinese characters on army caps and collar badges. Inaugurated in 1927 and once marked by enormous parades, it is now played out mainly in the official media.

Right: Longqing Ice Lantern Festival

September/October

The Mid-Autumn Festival again depends on when the moon reaches its fullest, usually around mid-September. Shops do a roaring trade in 'moon' cakes, round pastries filled with combinations of sesame paste, nuts, red beans, dried fruit, etc.

Late September is normally when the Chinese celebrate the memory of Confucius. Beijing's Temple of Confucius (Kong Miao) has revived the annual ceremony. As Confucius is China's most famous teacher, the event has been combined with Teachers' Day.

October 1 is the birthday of the People's Republic of China (PRC). National Day was formerly celebrated with a two-day public holiday but since 1999 the holiday is seven days. Again, plan in advance if you are intending to travel during this period. Five- and 10-year anniversaries have been accompanied by grandiose fireworks exhibitions and performances by dancers in Tiananmen Square. In other years, government buildings, road junctions and hotels are decked out in lights and flower arrangements. In the third week of October, when the weather is almost always glorious, the city hosts the Beijing International Marathon.

November/December

These are quiet, cold months in northern China, but Christmas is gaining momentum as a celebration for both consumers, Christians and curious onlookers. It is now trendy to exchange Christmas cards and gifts, while in shopping areas, Santa makes the odd appearance. Most large hotels have special meals and events promotions. Even small restaurants now put up Christmas decorations, which often remain in place until after Spring Festival the following year.

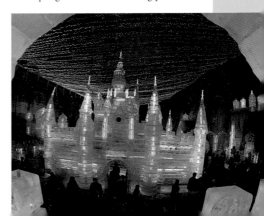

Practical Information

GETTING THERE

By Air

Beijing's Capital Airport, 30km (18 miles) from the centre, connects the city to all parts of China and to the world's major cities. In November 1999, the new and modern terminal building was opened. Airport inquiries at tel: 2580 or www.caft.com.

Capital Airport has connections to around 50 other cities in China. You must check in at least 30 minutes before departure for a domestic flight (although delays are common) and at least one hour before departure for an international flight. For shorter journeys within China, the train is often a better bet. Passengers leaving China by air must pay a 90-yuan airport tax, those taking domestic flights must pay 50 yuan.

Taxis are on the left as you leave the terminal. Make sure the taxi driver uses the meter, unless you have agreed on a price in advance (not advised, as you will almost certainly be paying too much). The journey to the city centre takes 30 minutes if the traffic is light, but can take an hour at busier times. Air China operates bus services to several places in Beijing, including its offices near Xidan, west of Tiananmen Square; the Lufthansa Centre; and the Beijing International Hotel, close to Beijing Railway Station. Many big hotels offer limousine or minibus services.

Domestic Airlines

China's national tourist offices and travel agencies, including hotel travel desks, can give you the current flight schedule of domestic airlines. You can buy tickets from travel agencies or airline booking offices. Travel agencies may be more convenient: although they charge more, they are more likely to have English speaking staff. Try Fesco Air Services, 1st Floor, China World Trade Centre; tel: 10-6505 3330. Or try CITS (*see page 89*), or China Youth Travel Service (CYTS).

Left: well-organised bicycle park
Right: Beijing is well-connected by air

By Rail

Beijing has two main railway stations: Beijing Station (Beijing Zhan) and Beijing West (Xi Zhan). Some trains to other parts of China run from the city's three smaller stations. Trans-Siberian trains leave from Beijing Station, the start of a fascinating five-day (via Mongolia) or six-day (via Northeast China) journey to Moscow. The Beijing International Hotel (9 Jianguomennei Dajie; tel: 10-6512 0507) has an international train ticket booking office.

If you are arriving on the Trans-Siberian, the same health and customs procedures apply as for international arrivals by air. Taxis are plentiful at Beijing Station, but beware of drivers who try to shepherd you into their cars before you reach the taxi stand; they will probably demand outlandish prices when you reach your destination. Less expensive, although usually very crowded, are buses which will take you downtown for only 2 yuan.

For travel within China, the best place to buy tickets is the foreigners' booking office to the left of the main concourse inside Beijing Station, where you can also buy tickets for trains leaving from Beijing West Station. Beijing West also has a foreigners' booking office. If you want a sleeper berth, especially in summer, buy your ticket at least five days in advance. Return tickets can be purchased for Hong Kong–Beijing, but not other routes.

By Road

Long-distance buses connect Beijing with many cities. These include Tianjin, Chengde, Beidaihe and Taiyuan. On some routes taking the bus is faster, but generally less comfort-

able, than trains. The sleeper buses operate on longer routes. Buses are recommended for shorter journeys, to places like Tianjin (two hours) or Chengde (four hours). Beijing's main long-distance bus stations are at Dongzhimen, Xizhimen and Yongdingmen.

TRAVEL ESSENTIALS

When to Visit
The best time to visit Beijing is from early September through to late November, when it's normally dry and sunny, with moderate temperatures. If you visit between March and May, chances are you'll encounter at least one of the annual dust storms that blow off the Gobi Desert. Summers are hot and often humid, with occasional torrential downpours. The hottest month, July, averages 26°C (79°F) but temperatures occasionally soar to nearly 40°C (104°F). Beijing winters are cold but mostly sunny. The coldest month, January, averages about -5°C (23°F), but temperatures can drop to as low as -23°C (-9°F). Locals wear several layers of clothing all winter, but fear not – one of the best buys in China is silk thermal underwear.

Visas and Passports
Valid passports and visas are required for all foreign tourists. Visas may be obtained at embassies or consulates of the People's Republic of China, or through overseas offices of the state-run China International Travel Service.

Most group tourists are allowed entry through group visas. For individual travellers, single-entry visas are valid for entry within three months of issue. Visas are usually issued for 30 to 60 days, and can be extended for another 30 days in China for a small fee at the foreign affairs section of Public Security Bureau at Andinmendong Dajie, tel: 10-8401 5297.

Business or study visas are issued on presentation of a letter or similar official document from any recognised Chinese organisation. Business travellers can be issued with multi-entry visas that are valid for six months to one year.

Carry your passport with you at all times, as it will often be required for checking into hotels, making reservations, changing money, and for bank transactions. If your passport is lost or stolen, contact your embassy immediately, and also the Public Security Bureau.

Customs
Written declarations are required only for visitors carrying more than US$5,000, or who exceed duty-free limits. Chinese customs are especially sensitive to pornographic material and publications deemed to be anti-government. You may be required to hand in your video tapes overnight for an inspection. Foreigners carrying illicit drugs have been sentenced to long prison terms.

Electricity
Electrical current runs at 220 volts. Many hotels have 110-volt shaver sockets.

Time
Beijing time is eight hours ahead of Greenwich Mean Time (GMT).

GETTING ACQUAINTED

Geography
Beijing municipality covers 16,808 sq km (6,488 sq miles). To its south is the fertile North China Plain and to the east, the Bohai Sea. To the west, northwest and northeast are mountain ranges.

Government and Economy
Beijing is the capital of the People's Republic of China; the Chinese Communist Party (CCP) centre of operations is headed by Jiang Zemin, who is also President. Premier Zhu Rongzi is Prime Minister. The 3,000-strong legislative body, the National People's Congress (NPC) meets annually in Beijing. In theory, the NPC can approve or reject legislation, but it is widely regarded as a rubber-stamp parliament. Real power lies with the seven members, including Jiang Zemin and Zhu Rongzi, of the Standing Committee of the CCP Politburo (sometimes known as China's cabinet). But personal connections and bureaucracy remain key features of day-to-day government and civil service operations.

Right: locals relax in Tiananmen Square

Beijing is one of four municipalities (along with Shanghai, Tianjin and, since 1997, Chongqing) with status equal to that of China's provinces. It is divided into 10 separate administrative districts. The city's local government set-up mirrors that of the central government; it is led by the Communist Party with limited participation by non-party officials.

China's economy is in transition from socialism to a 'socialist market economy'. Beijing is still well behind many southern and coastal cities in encouraging capitalism. The city is striving to catch up by modelling itself on Singapore. Places such as banks and post offices are still in the grip of the old system, but the new system is especially evident in the huge number of privately run restaurants.

Religion

For most of the period of Communist rule since 1949, worship of all kinds was discouraged or actively suppressed. Since 1978, the main religions have been allowed to revive, but most urban Chinese are atheists. Buddhism, Taoism, Islam and Christianity are all practised in temples, mosques and churches around Beijing.

Evangelising outside these institutions is forbidden and all religious groups are supposed to register with the government. Even so, Beijing has some underground (ie unregistered) Christian groups.

How Not To Offend

Chinese people are generally polite, especially when receiving guests or meeting business contacts, but the sheer weight of numbers means that things like queuing and other niceties are low priorities in towns and cities. Be firm but remain calm, even if you start to feel frustrated. Making a public scene sometimes engenders resentment and may not help you achieve what you want. Dining in China has its own etiquette, but no one will be offended if you start with the wrong dish or let food slip from your chopsticks. But do avoid eating with your fingers or licking them.

Population

Beijing has a population of 11.2 million, making it China's second-largest city after Shanghai (13.5 million). The majority Han people make up about 97 percent of the population. Of the 300,000 minority people in the city, about half are Muslims. As many as three million migrant workers from other parts of the country and around 100,000 foreigners live in Beijing.

MONEY MATTERS

Currency

In 1994, China abolished its dual currency system, making life simpler for visitors. Prices are in renminbi (RMB or 'people's

currency') yuan. Hotel rates are often cited in US dollars, but can be paid in renminbi. Foreign currency can be exchanged for renminbi at banks, the Friendship Store and some big shopping centres.

When you change money, you get a receipt that allows you to change renminbi back to foreign currency within six months. However, you can only change back up to 50 percent of the original sum.

Chinese money is counted in yuan, jiao and fen. One yuan is 100 fen or 10 jiao; one jiao is 10 fen. Colloquially, a yuan is usually called a kuai and a jiao is called a mao. Bills are denominated in 1, 2 and 5 jiao, and 1, 2, 5, 10, 20, 50 and 100 yuan. There are also 1 yuan, 5 jiao and 1 jiao coins, plus almost worthless 1, 2 and 5 fen coins.

Credit Cards

Major credit and charge cards like Diner's Club, Federal Card, American Express, MasterCard, Visa and JCB are accepted at all but low-budget hotels. Restaurants and stores geared toward tourism also accept them, but department stores that serve mainly Chinese customers do not.

Money Changers

Since Chinese renminbi is not fully convertible to foreign currency, there is a small black market for foreign currency.

The main reason why the black market still persists is because it is technically illegal for most Chinese businesses to conduct foreign currency transactions, so they obtain foreign currency through illegal channels.

The black market exchange rates are little more than those in banks and hotels, so changing money illegally on the street is no longer worth the hassle, or the risk of being cheated or even arrested (the latter is unlikely, but you could be the unlucky victim of a sudden police crackdown).

If you do choose to change money on the black market, avoid money-changers who try to rush you, who ask you to walk into a back street with them, or who are not obviously connected with a store. These people are often very good at sleight of hand. The 'safest' places to change money illegally are at the stores and market stalls.

Price Differences

In 1996, China officially abolished the practice of charging foreigners higher prices for hotels, entrance to tourist sites and so on. Most places have complied, resulting in large price rises for Chinese visitors. But vendors at markets, food stands and privately-run restaurants often try to charge foreigners more, as in many countries. The best way to deal with this is to find out local prices as soon as possible and insist on paying them, or walk away. If you are unsure of prices in a restaurant, find out the prices of individual dishes before ordering them.

Tipping

In Chairman Mao's time, tipping was thought of as a bourgeois affectation. For better or worse, some hotel staff have come to expect tips, especially bell boys and restroom attendants. Taxi drivers and door attendants do not expect tips. Restaurants catering to foreigners usually add a 10 or 15 percent service charge to the bill.

GETTING AROUND

Taxis

Beijing is oversupplied with taxis, which are inexpensive and convenient. Smaller cars cost 1.20 or 1.60 yuan per kilometre. Larger cars cost 2 or 3 yuan per kilometre. Always make sure the metre is switched on before setting off. A few taxi drivers speak English but it is a good idea to carry the name and address of your hotel (name cards in Chinese are very useful for this) and ensure that your destination is written in Chinese before setting off. Drivers must post their car number and iden-

Left: taxis display signs denoting cost
Top right: busy subway station

tity card inside the taxi, so you can note down these details in case of complaints. While taxi drivers must attend English classes once a week (as the city prepares for the 2008 Olympics), the English ability of most drivers is currently non-existent.

Beijing's taxi drivers are generally honest. Do not assume the worst if they take convoluted routes. The city's many one-way streets and complex traffic rules forbid left turns at many junctions. But drivers who line up for hours in front of hotels are often hoping for big fares.

Taxis can also be rented for longer trips, such as whole-day tours or visits to the Great Wall or Ming Tombs. If you plan to do this, make sure you agree to the total fare and

the precise itinerary in advance. Call Capital Taxi (tel: 10-6513 8893); Beijing Taxi (tel: 10-6837 3399); or Beijing Bashi (tel: 10-6779 7514).

Bus

Beijing's intricate and changing bus network can be a mystery even to lifelong residents of the city. Buses are slow and crowded and the distances between stops are sometimes long – but they are very inexpensive and are worth taking for short journeys. A few routes have now been improved, with air-conditioned double-decker buses. Minibuses ply the same routes as the buses, but offer a faster, more comfortable service at several times the ordinary bus fare, though prices are still low by Western standards.

Subway

The city's subway system is limited to just two lines, but provides a useful link between Beijing Station and some major tourist areas, such as Tiananmen Square, Yonghegong and Kong Miao temples and the Drum and Bell Towers. It gets crowded during rush hour, though it is generally preferable to the bus. Recordings in English and Chinese announce the stops. Buy your ticket (2 or 3 yuan to any destination) when you enter the subway station.

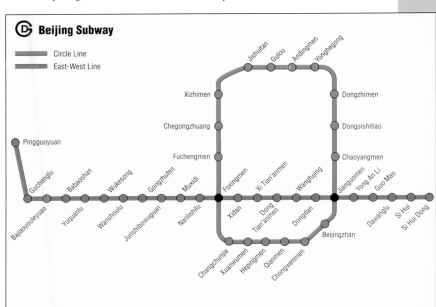

Beijing Subway

Circle Line
East-West Line

Jishuitan · Gulou · Andingmen · Yonghegong
Xizhimen · Dongzhimen
Chegongzhuang · Dongsishitiao
Fuchengmen · Chaoyangmen
Pingguoyuan · Guchenglu · Babaoshan · Wukesong · Gongzhufen · Muxidi · Fuxingmen · Xi Tian'anmen · Wangfujing · Jianguomen · Yong An Li · Guo Mao · Si Hui · Si Hui Dong
Bajiaoyoulequan · Yuquanlu · Wanshoulu · Junshibowuguan · Nanlishilu · Xidan · Dong Tian'anmen · Dongdan · Dawanglu
Changchunjie · Xuanwumen · Hepingmen · Qianmen · Chongwenmen · Beijingzhan

Cars

Rental cars come with drivers and can be hired from most hotels. Negotiate for half- and whole-day rates. Foreign tourists are not allowed to drive in China, unless given special permission.

Try the following companies: Beijing Minibus Co (tel: 10-6721 1558); Beijing Transport Co Service for Foreigners (tel: 10-6502 2616); Beijing Capital Auto Group (tel: 10-6775 0039); or Today New Concept Car Rental (tel: 10-6237 0138).

Bicycles

Cycling is the most enjoyable way to see Beijing, but it requires steady nerves and basic fitness. If you are not used to urban cycling, it is a good idea to get some practice before going to China.

Many hotels have bicycles for hire: Hua Qiao Hotel (deposit 500 yuan, 100 yuan for whole day); Great Wall Hotel (deposit between 400 and 1000 yuan, 20–35 yuan per hour); Jing Lun Hotel (deposit 600 yuan, 50 yuan per day). Beijingers ride all year round, through all kinds of weather, even on snow and ice.

Pedicabs

If you want to experience travelling through Beijing at a cyclist's pace but don't feel up to cycling yourself, pedicabs – three-wheeled bicycles that accommodate up to two passengers at the back plus the driver in front – can be hired near many tourist sites and larger hotels. Some hotels have their own pedicabs at set prices. Generally, prices are negotiable from 5 to 30 yuan, depending on the distance you wish to go and the time of day. A ride from the Friendship Store to Tiananmen Square, about 4km (2½ miles), will cost you around 20 yuan, for example.

You'll find that pedicabs are often more expensive than taxis, but as Beijing's rush hour traffic jams worsen by the day, it is sometimes faster to walk, cycle or hop into a pedicab rather than take a taxi to a nearby destination.

If you are interested in taking a pedicab tour of Beijing's *hutong* (alleys), you can arrange this with the Hutong Pedicab Company. The company is located at 26 Dianmen Nei Xidajie; tel: 10-6612-3236.

HOURS AND HOLIDAYS

Business Hours

Business hours vary. Government offices, including banks, are generally open 8am–5pm. Some close earlier and most have a lunch break from noon–1pm. Offices also open on Saturday mornings, but not on Sundays. The best time to get things done is at the start of the working day.

Most shops open at 9am and close around 9pm, though if they are still state run they can close by 6pm. Many department stores and privately run small stores open until 9pm. Money exchange outlets (but not banks) are open seven days a week and generally operate long hours. At the tourist sites, ticket sales may stop 30 minutes before closing time and many museums are closed on Mondays.

ACCOMMODATION

Luxury hotels abound in Beijing, with the construction of many more in progress, in anticipation of the Beijing Olympics in 2008. There are few bargains, mainly due to the state-set minimums on room rates. Hotels marked JV are joint ventures run by foreign management, which often means they offer better service at higher cost. Rates at all but the budget hotels are subject to 10–15 percent tax and service charges. The published hotel rates for a standard double room are categorised as follows:

$$$$ = US$200 and up;
$$$ = US$150–200;
$$ = US$100–150;
$ = US$50–100

Beijing

$$$$

China World Hotel
1 Jianguomenwai Dajie, Chaoyang East
Tel: 10-6505 2266
Fax: 10-6505 167
www.shangri-la.com
Top class service and accommodations, with health club, swimming pool, shopping and business centres, plus several Western and Asian restaurants. It is well located for business travellers.

Diaoyutai State Guest House
Sanlihe Lu, east of Yuyuantan Park
Tel: 10-6859 1188
Fax: 10-6851 3362
www.chinadyt.com
Once reserved for senior Chinese officials and state guests, this hotel is still used to accommodate VIPs. As a result, expect high security and high prices.

Grand Hotel Beijing
35 Dongchang'an Jie, Dongcheng
Tel: 10-6513 7788
Fax: 10-6513 0049
www.grandhotelbeijing.com
e-mail: sales@grandhotelbeijing.com
This Hong Kong joint venture, attached to the Beijing Hotel, offers the height of luxury a stone's throw from Tiananmen Square. Its facilities include a rooftop terrace with views over the square.

Hilton Hotel
1 Dongfang Lu, Dongsanhuan Beilu,
Chaoyang Northeast
Tel: 10-6466 2288
Fax: 10-6465 3052
email: reserve@hiltonbeijing.com.cn
Next to the airport expressway, this has, like all Hiltons, every comfort. Among the highlights are Japanese and Cajun restaurants.

Palace Hotel
8 Jinyu Hutong, Wangfujing Dajie,
Dongcheng
Tel: 10-6512 8899
Fax: 10-6512 9050
Modern, functional hotel with Chinese imperial flourishes. A waterfall cascades down into a lobby full of Chinese antiques, while designer labels compete in the shopping arcade. Located in a lively street ideal for shopping.

Shangri-La Hotel
29 Zizhuyuan Lu, Haidian
Tel: 10-6841 2211
Fax: 10-6841 8006
www.shangri-la.com
This tasteful high-rise hotel has meeting rooms, a ballroom, French and Asian restaurants and a full range of other facilities. On the western edge of the city, it provides a shuttle-bus service to downtown areas.

$$$
Beijing Hotel
33 Dongchang'an Jie, Dongcheng
Tel: 10-6513 7766
Fax: 10-6513 7703, 6513 7307
e-mail: business@chinabeijinghotel.com.cn
Opened in 1917, with a long list of famous guests, this is still considered one of the best hotels in Beijing. Period features give it an air of tradition, in contrast to many newer competitors. Centrally located, on the corner of Wangfujing shopping street.

Beijing International Club Hotel
21 Jianguomenwai Dajie, Chaoyang East
Tel: 10-6460 6688
Fax: 10-6460 3299
Matching Chinese tradition with modern furniture, this chic hotel opened in late 1997 in a prime location behind the International Club. The hotel's elegant Press Club Bar quickly became a favourite of the foreign business community.

practical information

health club, restaurants and the authentic German Paulaner Brauhaus restaurant and pub.

Peace Hotel
3 Jinyu Hutong, Wangfujing Dajie, Dongcheng
Tel: 10-6512 8833
Fax: 10-6512 6863
In the same lively street as the Palace Hotel, close to Tiananmen and the Imperial Palace, this joint venture provides spacious rooms.

Traders' Hotel
1 Jianguomenwai Dajie, Chaoyang East
Tel: 10-6505 2277
Fax: 10-6505 3144
www.shangri-la.com
Well located at the northern end of the China World Trade Centre business complex. With solid service, food and accommodations, this is a less expensive option than the neighbouring China World Hotel.

$$
Beijing Bamboo Garden Hotel
24 Xiaoshiqiao Hutong, Jiugulou Dajie
Tel: 10-6403 2229
Fax: 10-6401 2633
Simple, clean rooms open onto a classical Chinese garden, close to the Drum Tower. What it lacks in facilities compared with large, modern hotels, it more than compensates for in atmosphere.

Beijing International Hotel
19 Jianguomenwai Dajie, Dongcheng
Tel: 10-6512 6688
Fax: 10-6512 9961
With a good location near Beijing Station and the Henderson and Cofco Plaza shopping centres, this 1,000-room hotel offers full facilities, including booking offices for international flights and trains.

Dragon Spring Hotel
Shuizha Beilu, Mentougou
Tel: 10-6984 3366, 6984 3362
Fax: 10-6984 4377
For atmosphere and facilities, this international hotel built in classical Chinese style beats most similarly priced hotels in Beijing. But it is located near the Western Hills, an hour from the city centre.

Gloria Plaza Hotel
2 Jianguomen Nandajie, Chaoyang East
Tel: 10-6515 8855
Fax: 10-6515 8533
www.hotel-web.com/gloria/beijing
With a great location on a major junction, opposite the Ancient Observatory and next to one of the main CITS offices, the Gloria Plaza has several restaurants and a lively sports bar.

Holiday Inn Crowne Plaza
48 Wangfujing Dajie, Dengshikou, Dongcheng
Tel: 10-6513 3388
Fax: 10-6513 2513
www.crowneplaza.com
email: hicpb@public3.bta.net.cn
Located on one of central Beijing's busiest shopping streets, close to the Imperial Palace, the Crowne Plaza has its own gallery of modern Chinese art and a salon for performances of traditional Chinese music.

Kempinski Hotel
50 Liangmaqiao Lu, Beijing Lufthansa Centre, Chaoyang Northeast
Tel: 10-6465 3388
Fax: 10-6465 3366
www.kempinski_beijing.com
email: khblc.public.east.cn.net
Attached to Friendship (Youyi) Shopping City, this hotel has all facilities, including

Above: lobby, Holiday Inn Crowne Plaza
Right: bar at the Kempinski Hotel

Fragrant Hills Hotel
inside Fragrant Hills Park
Tel: 10-6259 1166
Fax: 10-6259 1762
A modern sanctuary from the urban hustle and bustle, in the lush hills northwest of Beijing, beyond the Summer Palace. There is a swimming pool and Chinese and Western restaurants.

Friendship Hotel
3 Baishiqiao Lu, Haidian
Tel: 10-6849 8888
Fax: 10-6849 8866
www.cbw.com/hotel/friendship
Part of a huge state-run hotel spread out in pleasant grounds close to the Summer Palace and university district, the hotel has several sections offering a range of prices and facilities. It is also home to many foreigners working for Chinese state employers.

Jing Guang New World Hotel
Hujia Lou, Dongsanhuan Lu,
Chaoyang East
Tel: 10-6597 8888
Fax: 10-6597 3333
A 53-storey building dominating the eastern Third Ring Road, the Jing Guang New World is almost a self-contained town, with its own bakery, restaurants, nightclubs, children's play areas, medical centre and supermarket – and, of course, some of the best views of Beijing.

Twenty-First Century Hotel
40 Liangmaqiao Lu, Chaoyang
Tel: 10-6466 3311
Fax: 10-6466 3311
www.21st.cn.net
e-mail: sale@21st.cn.net
Just 1 km (½ mile) east of the Lufthansa Centre, this hotel is part of a modern complex including shops, a small Internet centre, Korean, Chinese and Western restaurants, business facilities, theatres and a movie house. Several lively bars are across the road.

Ziyu (Purple Jade) Hotel
55 Xisanhuan Beilu, Xicheng
Tel: 10-6841 1188
Fax: 10-6841 1355
Through a traditional gateway, you enter a compound containing both ancient and modern architectural styles. Traditional rooms enclose small courtyard gardens, while the main block has Western-style rooms with full facilities. Situated in Beijing's western suburbs, the Ziyu is convenient for Beijing West Railway Station, the Summer Palaces and the Fragrant Hills.

$
Beifang Hotel
45 Dongdan Beidajie, Dongcheng
Tel: 10-6525 2831
Fax: 10-6525 2928
Retaining touches of traditional Chinese architecture, this small hotel was completed

in 1953. It is conveniently located in the city centre near Wangfujing, and has a restaurant serving delicious Beifang (northern) Chinese dishes.

Haoyuan Hotel
Shijia Hutong, Dongsinan Dajie, Dongcheng
Tel: 10-6512 5557
Fax: 10-6525 3179
Hidden away in a narrow alley near the busy Dongdan shopping street and close to the Palace Hotel, the Haoyuan's rooms surround two quiet courtyards. The buildings are a traditional combination of brick and red lacquered wood, with curved tiles on the roofs. A small restaurant serves hearty traditional fare at very reasonable prices.

Jinghua Hotel
Xiluoyuan Nanlu Nan Sanhuan, Yangqiao
Tel: 10-6722 2211
Fax: 10-6721 1455
The cheap-and-cheerful Jinghua is in the far south of Beijing, on the Third Ring Road. Though this is a backpacker favourite, the rooms have showers, telephones and air-conditioners. Dormitory beds are also available.

Longtan Hotel
15 Panjiayuan Nanlu, Second Ring Road South
Tel: 10-6771 1602
Fax: 10-6771 4028
This has long been a favourite with budget travellers who want to get away from the more crowded backpacker hotels. Situated opposite Longtan Park in the south of the city, its facilities are basic and it is away from the tourist areas, but this modern hotel offers relatively inexpensive comforts. Single travellers are usually allowed to share rooms with either three or four beds.

Lusongyuan Hotel
22 Banchang Hutong, Kuanjie, Dongcheng
Tel: 10-6401 1116
Fax: 10-6403 0418
This courtyard hotel was established in 1980 in a former Qing dynasty official's residence. Rooms are refined and airy. Stone lions still guard the traditional wooden gate, which leads to the pavilions, trees, rockeries and potted plants that fill the courtyards. The Chinese restaurant gets some good reviews.

Outside Beijing
Chengde
Qianwanglou Hotel
Bifengmen Lu
Tel: 0314-202 4385
For atmosphere alone this is the best option in Chengde. The small, exquisitely refurbished hotel occupies a Qing dynasty mansion set just inside the grounds of the imperial resort. **$$**

Yunshan Hotel
6 Nanyuan Jie
Tel: 0314-202 4657
This is the main tourist hotel in Chengde, close to the station and with some of the best facilities. **$$**

Mongolian Yurt Holiday Village
Tel: 0314-216 2710
In summer, the least expensive option is a *yurt* (circular felt tent), located inside the grounds of the imperial resort. You don't have to rough it too much, as the *yurts* have their own washrooms and TVs, and are air-conditioned. High on the kitsch factor. **$**

Above: Gloria Plaza Hotel

Beidaihe/Shanhaiguan

Beidaihe Guesthouse for Diplomatic Missions
1 Baosan Lu, Beidaihe
Tel: 0335-404 1807
(or 10-6532 4336 in Beijing)
Just five minutes from the main beach, this hotel has friendly staff and a good seafood restaurant. All rooms have balconies with fine sea views. **$$**

Jinshan Guesthouse
4 Dongsan Lu, Beidaihe
Tel: 0335-404 1338
Fax: 0335-404 2478
On a quieter stretch of beach, approximately 4 km (2½ miles) north of the town centre, the Jinshan has full facilities, including a business centre and a bowling alley. **$$**

Jingshan Hotel
Dong Dajie, Shanhaiguan
Tel: 0335-505 1130
Next to the famous East Gate of the Shanhaiguan garrison on the Great Wall, the Jingshan has comfortable rooms in the heart of the small town. **$**

HEALTH AND EMERGENCIES

Hygiene/General Health
Tap water should always be boiled before drinking. Some hotels have water purification systems and all sell bottled water and provide flasks of boiled water in guest rooms. Bottled water and canned soft drinks are available at tourist sites and on most streets.

Although they are not necessarily unsafe, avoid ice cream, yoghurt and drinks from large vats. If buying food from street vendors, make sure it is hot and freshly cooked and served in clean dishes, preferably disposable. Avoid restaurants with dirty utensils or poor food handling practices to avoid contracting hepatitis, which is endemic. And wash your hands frequently. Outside the hotels, most toilets are the crude squat type. Better public restrooms require a small fee. Carry your own toilet paper.

Colds and stomach disorders are the most common travellers' complaints. Attention to

hygiene goes a long way to preventing both. Medicines that may come in handy are Panadol, Lomotil (or Imodium), general antibiotics, Pepto-Bismol and aspirin. The Watson's drugstore in the Palace Hotel has a wide selection of Western medicines. Malaria prevention is not necessary for Beijing or anywhere in northern China. If you're planning an extended visit to China, consult your doctor about vaccinations.

Medical Services
In case of dire emergency, dial 120 for an ambulance; or you can try MEDEX Assistance (Lufthansa Centre, Regus Office 19; tel: 10-6465 1264) or SOS Assistance (1 Xinfusancun Beijie; Beixinzulin Zhongxin; tel: 10-6462 9100). Two of the best hospitals for foreigners are the Sino-Japanese Friendship Hospital (north end of Heping Lu; tel: 10-6529 5812, 6422 1122) and the Peking Union Medical Hospital (53 Dongdanbei Dajie; emergency tel: 10-6529 5284). The International Medical Clinic (Room 106 Regus Office Building, Lufthansa Centre; tel: 10-6465 1561, 6465 1562) is an outpatient clinic geared to foreigners.

COMMUNICATIONS AND NEWS

Mail
Hotel desks provide the most convenient service for posting letters and parcels. The International Post Office (open 8am–6.30pm; tel: 10-6512-8114) on Yabao Lu, about 300m (330yds) north of the Jianguomen junction, handles international mail and is Beijing's *poste restante* address.

Telephone
Major hotels have IDD service available in the rooms, and smaller hotels usually have business centres with IDD. In shopping areas there are cardphone booths: cards are normally available in 20, 50, 100 and 200 yuan units. China's IDD rates have been reduced but remain high by world standards, and hotels usually add a service charge. US credit phone card access codes from China are as follows. Sprint tel: 108-13; AT&T tel: 108-11; MCI/Worldphone tel: 108-12. Fax, cable,

e-mail and Internet services are also widely available in hotels.

Another option is the International Post Office *(see Mail on page 87)*. Besides long-distance calls, it handles remittances, money orders and telegraphic money transfers.

The Long-Distance Telephone Building at Fuxingmennei Dajie (8.30am–6pm) handles long-distance, conference and pre-booked telephone calls. The Telex Building on West Dongchang'an Jie (24 hours) has a complete range of telephone and fax services.

Local telephone calls can be made from streetside booths with attendants, and also from many stores. Local calls usually cost 5 jiao. You will find that coin-operated phones are often out of order.

The country code for calling China is 86, and the area code for Beijing is 10.

Courier Services

Express courier services in Beijing include DHL (tel: 800-810 8000), Federal Express (tel: 800-810 2338, 6468 5566), TNT (tel: 10-6465 2227 ext 258/259) and UPS (tel: 10-6581 2088 ext 1).

Media

The English-Language *China Daily* reports domestic and foreign news with an official slant. The *International Herald Tribune,* *Asian Wall Street Journal* and international news magazines are all available.

Most major hotels offer CNN's 24-hour programmes. Star TV from Hong Kong is also available. China Central Television broadcasts English-language news on CCTV 4 at 7–7.30pm; CCTV 9 has English language news all day while local programmes and most imported programmes are broadcast in Chinese. Local radio broadcasts in English and other languages can be heard on 91.5FM and 87.5FM.

USEFUL INFORMATION

Tourist Information and Websites

The Beijing Tourism Administration operates a hotline for emergencies and information, tel: 10-6513 0828. The English spoken at the other end is not always perfect, but if you are away from your hotel, it is worth a try. Most hotels have their own travel desks for arranging cars and tours. Make good use of the information desk or concierge to check on events and opening and closing times. English-language publications listing ongoing events are available in hotels: *China Daily*, *Beijing Weekend*, BLT, *Beijing This Month*, *Beijing Info* and the quarterly *Welcome to China*.

Above: old post office, Dongliaominxian

For information on travel elsewhere in China, your best bet is to start with your hotel's travel office. Or contact China International Travel Service (CITS) (tel: 10-6601 1122). This is China's main state-run tourism bureau, with branches throughout the country. CITS has a website at www.cits.com.cn.

Useful websites sponsored by Beijing Tourism Administration and other government bodies include:
www.bta.gov.cn
www.chinatour.com
www.beijingtour.net.cn
www.cbw.com

Foreign Airline Offices

Air France: Room 512 Feng Lian Tower; tel: 10-6588 1388
Alitalia: 5/F West Wing China World Trade Centre; tel: 10-6505 6657
All Nippon Airways: 1/F Fa Zhan Tower, Dongshanhuan Beilu; tel: 10-6590 9191
Asiana Airlines: Room 102 Lufthansa Centre; tel: 10-6468 4000
British Airways: Room 210 Scitech Tower; tel: 10-6512 4070
Canadian Airlines: Room 201 Lufthansa Centre; tel: 10-6468 2001
Dragonair: Room 1710 Heng Ji Centre; tel: 10-6518 2533
Finnair: Room 102 Scitech Tower; tel: 10-6512 7180
Japan Airlines: Hotel New Otani, Chang Fu Gong Office Building; tel: 10-6513 0888
KLM: Room 501 China World Trade Centre; tel: 10-6505 3505
Korean Air: 401 West Wing, China World Trade Centre; tel: 10-6505 0088
Lufthansa: Beijing Lufthansa Centre; tel: 10-6465 4488

Malaysian Airlines: 10/F China World Trade Centre; tel: 10-6505 2681
Northwest Airlines: Room 104 China World Trade Centre; tel: 10-6505 3505
SAS: Room 1403 Heng Ji Centre; tel: 10-6518 3738
Singapore Airlines: 8/F China World Trade Centre; tel: 10-6505 2233
Swissair: 6/F Scitech Tower; tel: 10-6512 3555
United Airlines: 1/F Office Building Lufthansa Centre; tel: 10-6463 1111

Embassies

Australia: 21 Dongzhimen Wai Dajie; tel: 10-6532 4349; fax: 10-6532 2331
Canada: 19 Dongzhimen Wai Dajie; tel: 10-6532 3536; fax: 10-6532 1684
France: 3 Dongsan Jie, Sanlitun; tel: 10-6532 1331; fax: 10-6532 4757
Germany: 5 Dongzhimen Wai Dajie; tel: 10-6532 2161; fax: 10-6532 5336
Italy: 2 Dong'er Jie, Sanlitun; tel: 10-6532 2131; fax: 10-6532 4676
Japan: 7 Ritian Lu, Jianguomen Wai; tel: 10-6532 2361; fax: 10-6532 4625
Netherlands: 4 Lingmahe Nanlu; tel: 10-6532 1131; fax: 10-6532 4689
New Zealand: Dong'er Jie, Ritan Lu; tel: 10-6532 2731; fax: 10-6532 4689
Norway: 1 Dongyi Jie, Sanlitun; tel: 10-6532 2261; fax: 10-6532 2392
Russia: 4 Dongzhimenbei Zhongjie; tel: 10-6532 2051; fax: 10-6532 1267
Singapore: 27/F Kerry Centre, Guanghua Lu; tel: 10-8529 6256; fax: 10-8529 6247
South Korea: 4/F China World Trade Centre; tel: 10-6532 0290; fax: 10-6532 0141
Spain: 9 Sanlitun Lu; tel: 10-6532 1986; fax: 10-6532 3401
Sweden: 3 Dongzhimen Wai Dajie; tel: 10-6532 3331; fax: 10-6532 2909
Switzerland: Dongwu Jie, Sanlitun; tel: 10-6532 2736; fax: 10-6532 4353
Thailand: 40 Guanghua Lu; tel: 10-6532 1903; fax: 10-6532 3890
United Kingdom: 21/F North Tower Kerry Centre, 1 Guanghua Lu; tel: 10-8529 6077; fax: 10-6532 1939
United States: 2 Xiushuidong Jie, Jianguomenwai; tel: 10-6532 3831; fax: 10-6532 3178

Left: Beijing's new telephone booths

LANGUAGE

Large hotels usually have many English-speaking staff. Outside of hotels, you'll find that most people speak only a little English. English, French, Japanese, Italian, German and Spanish interpreters can be employed through major hotels or CITS. Prices are negotiable depending on the group's size.

Useful Phrases

Hello/How are you?	Ni Hao?
Goodbye	Zai jian
Thank You	Xie xie
I'm sorry/Excuse me	Dui bu qi
No problem	Mei you wen ti
How much does it cost?	Duo shao qian?
Wait a moment	Deng yi xia
No, don't have	Mei you
It doesn't matter	Mei you guan xi
I want	Wo yao
Good	Hao
Bad	Bu hao
Not possible	Bu xing
restaurant	fan dian
taxi	chu zu qi che
telephone	dian hua
hotel	bin guan
train	huo che
airplane	fei ji
restroom	ce suo
north	bei
south	nan
east	dong
west	xi
middle	zhong
street	jie
avenue	dajie
road	lu
gate	men
outside	wai
inside	nei
one	yi
two	er
three	san
four	si
five	wu
six	liu
seven	qi
eight	ba
nine	jiu
ten	shi

FURTHER READING

China Pop: How Soap Operas, Tabloids and Bestsellers Are Transforming a Culture. Zha Jianying. New Press, 1995. Zha takes an off-beat look at the explosion of Chinese popular culture in the 1980s and 1990s.

China Remembers by Zhang Lijia and Calum MacLeod. Oxford University Press, 1999. A fascinating and accessible look at New China through the eyes of 33 people who have vivid memories of five decades.

China Wakes: The Struggle for the Soul of a Rising Power by Nicholas Kristof and Sheryl Wudunn. Random House, 1995. A Beijing correspondent and his wife detail personal experiences in China.

Hiking on History by William Lindesay. Oxford University Press, 2000. Indispensable for hikers, this is a guide to walking on several unrestored, less-visited sections of the Great Wall near Beijing.

In the Red, Geremie Barme, Columbia University Press, 1999. An academic examination of literary trends in China since 1989, especially the voices of dissent.

On a Chinese Screen by Somerset Maugham, Oxford University Press, 1997. Maugham, who first published this travelogue in 1922, wrote brief but engaging sketches of some of the local and foreign characters he met in Beijing.

Peking Opera by Colin MacKerras. Oxford University Press, 1997. A simple explanation of the history and standard forms of the art of Peking opera. Part of the Oxford Images of Asia series.

The Forbidden City: Centre of Imperial China (Discoveries) by Gilles Beguin and Dominique Morel. Abrams, 1997. A brief account details the daily lives of Ming and Qing emperors in the former imperial palace.

The Search for Modern China by Jonathan Spence. Norton, 1990. Bringing to life Chinese society and politics over the past 400 years, this has become a standard text for students of Chinese history.

Wild Swans: Three Daughters of China by Jung Chang. Anchor Books, 1991. Adding plenty of historical detail, Wild Swans records 20th-century China through the lives of three generations of women, starting with the author's concubine grandmother.

Right: toffee apples for sale

INSIGHT
Pocket Guides

Insight Pocket Guides pioneered a new approach to guidebooks, introducing the concept of the authors as "local hosts" who would provide readers with personal recommendations, just as they would give honest advice to a friend who came to stay. They also included a full-size pull-out map.

Now, to cope with the needs of the 21st century, new editions in this growing series are being given a new look to make them more practical to use, and restaurant and hotel listings have been greatly expanded.

☀ INSIGHT GUIDES

The world's largest collection of visual travel guides

Now in association with

ACKNOWLEDGEMENTS

Cover	**Paul Beiboer**
Backcover	**Marcus Wilson Smith/APA**
Photography	**Marcus Wilson Smith/APA and**
Pages 76	**Bodo Bondzio**
32T	**Lance Dawning**
15, 30, 41T/B, 45T, 48T, 52T, 59, 61, 63T/B, 73, 77	**Kari Huus**
67	**Catherine Karnow**
6T, 11, 12, 13, 14, 16	**Manfred Morgenstern**
28	**Erhard Pansegrau**
10, 51, 68	**Photobank**
60	**Panos Pictures**
23	**Andrea Pistolesi**
49	**David Sanger**
62	**Peter Scheckmann**
52B	**Machtelb Stikvoort**
54	**Tom Till**
32B	**Elke Wandel**
74, 75	**Xinhua News Agency**
Cartography	**Maria Donnelly**
Cover Design	**Carlotta Junger**
Production	**Caroline Low**

INDEX

index